www.twistedbadge.com

THE TWISTED BADGE

An inside look at politics in law enforcement

by

Mike Madigan

3rd Edition

INTEGRITY PUBLICATIONS

Published by:

Integrity Publications
23361 El Toro Road
Suite 106
Lake Forest, Ca. 92630
(949) 380-0205

Cover art by: Point Savannah, Graphic Design

Library of Congress Catalog Card
Number: 99-091142
ISBN: 0-924309-01-6

1st printing January 1989
2nd printing August 1989
3rd printing September 1990
4th printing February 1993
5th printing September 1995

Dedication

This book is dedicated to those criminal justice professionals who bring honor to the badge.

Thank you.

Contents

The episodes presented in this book are based, in part, upon the actual testimony and statements of witnesses and victims obtained during pending litigation. The author cannot attest to the truthfulness or correctness contained in the sworn testimony, but each individual knew that lying under oath could subject them to a charge of perjury. Other information has been obtained from newspaper articles, publications, interviews with persons directly involved in the story and from personal experience.

Characterizations of persons, places or things are the opinion of the author and those individuals making the statements.

Foreword

I am and have always been pro law enforcement, but as we become better equipped to identify and remove criminals from our communities, we face new challenges.

This book presents cases that may have been filed for the wrong reasons and others, including two homicides, which were never filed at all. Hopefully, you'll be able to judge for yourself whether justice has been served.

Whether you are in, out or considering a career in law enforcement, we must all be vigilant so that honest and ethical people can keep the shine on the badge.

* * *

Introduction

Did a candidate for Attorney General prosecute another candidate for publicity and political advantage? Criminal charges filed in 1996 against newly elected Assemblyman Scott Baugh were dismissed, re-filed, partially dismissed, then finally referred to the California Attorney General's Office. Things changed when it was discovered that the Capizzi for Attorney General campaign had accepted contributions from one of Assemblyman Baugh's political opponents, who also had served on his campaign Finance Committee!

Did a California Department of Justice investigator who shot his wife in the back of the head and a training officer who shot a deputy sheriff in the face get one free shot? No criminal charges were filed in either case.

Is your police chief dodging creditors? Is he using his city issued Master Card for personal shopping trips to Nordstrom's? Is he charging fine wines, expensive lunches and dinners with friends? He is if you live in the city of Bell Gardens, near Los Angeles. This same police chief is being sued for exposing a reserve officer who'd been working undercover at a local casino.

Have you ever been caught speeding in a radar trap? If you drive Interstate 40 from California to Arizona, you are entering a war zone where no "fuzz buster" will help you. Trained soldiers of the California Highway Patrol will use binoculars to see if you look like the enemy. If you do, or if they think you might, you're going down. Forget the Constitution. They will interrogate you, search your car and if possible, arrest you and take your possessions. Then they will lie on cue in court.

What went on behind the scenes in the largest municipal bankruptcy in US history? Was bankruptcy the only alternative?

Hindsight is perfect, but the conduct of those in power after the decision was made turned a financial crisis into a mean spirited nightmare for hard working civil servants.

In a very unusual legal proceeding, a DA shut down a grand jury investigation of Merrill Lynch in exchange for a payment of $30 million. About $3 million went to the DA's budget and in the years that followed, more than $1 million was spent on a very questionable political prosecution.

Much of the information obtained in these chapters came from sworn peace officers disgusted with "business as usual". They deserve our trust because to them, the badge is a symbol of honor, not power.

Honest and valuable people often get swept up by prosecutors with unlimited resources. If we're not vigilant, a prosecutor accountable to no one could become more powerful than the President of the United States.

In 1998, I was called for the third time in three years for jury duty. I wasn't selected, but I hope to sit as a juror sometime in the future. We should be proud and honored to serve. Nowadays, the general attitude seems to be that jury duty is a big hassle. How can unbiased law enforcement work if juries think evaluating evidence is nothing more than an intrusion?

My sincere wish is that your next contact with law enforcement and/or jury duty will be a positive experience.

The badge is not for twisting.

* * *

1

The Private Investigator

Most private investigators start out in law enforcement, but my path was a little different. At Hunter College I majored in Music and sang at funerals and weddings to support myself. I also bartended two nights a week on the upper east side of Manhattan. The funerals were always in the morning and I never really had to be in great voice. Fortunately for the happy couples, weddings were always later in the day.

In my senior year, another student and I were invited to study voice at the La Scala Opera House in Milan, Italy. A classmate's father was the Vice President of US Lines, so I made my first trip to Europe in luxury. Invited to sing at the Captain's Ball, dignitaries clapped politely as I sang in the tuxedo I'd rented for the occasion. When I got to Paris it dawned on me that I'd rented the tux in New York and it had to be back in a week!

The guys at the post office in Paris probably still tell the story of that "crayzee Amayreecan" who spent more than the tuxedo was worth to get it back on time. What the hell was I thinking? When we arrived at the Centro di Perfezionamente Artisti Lirici in the world famous Teatro Alla Scala, the Director said the class size had been reduced, so we'd have to audition. After our one and only appearance, we were ready to study with nowhere to go. At least we can each say we sang solos on that great stage.

My classmate was devastated. She returned to the states and I took a train to see Venice. From there I hitched a ride with an Austrian businessman who was on his way to Sofia, the capital of Bulgaria, but I overslept in Budapest and he left without me.

Because of the draft, I either had to be in school or the army, so I took the night train to Prague on my way back to the other side of the Iron Curtain.

That October night in 1968, Russia invaded Czechoslovakia. When I walked out of the train station, everyone seemed to be standing around in cafes eating pastries and drinking schnapps. Dazed workers watched tanks and heavy artillery clatter up and down the streets. Mean looking Mongolian soldiers paraded through the city. The main library and radio station had been shelled, so I walked around taking pictures - a lot of pictures. No one seemed to care.

The people at the hotel I'd booked were surprised to see me. I only had a transit visa and the manager said I'd better head west to Germany. Trains and buses were shut down, so the next morning I hitchhiked west until dark, then stopped at a tiny cafe. After I explained my situation, the sympathetic owners taped a paper Czech flag to the side of my suitcase. From then on, every car stopped and gave me a ride closer to the border.

When I got to the buffer zone it was almost midnight and the guards looked at me like I was a ghost. After inspecting my US passport, they said the border was closed. Then one of them said no cars could go through, but I could walk it. I thought I heard that phrase "crayzee Amayreecan" again as a walked into the night. Heavy equipment and tanks made incredible noise as I carried my Czech flagged suitcase the dark mile to Germany.

On the western side I came upon a small shack illuminated by a single bare light bulb. A thin, balding man was writing at a desk and when I knocked at the window, I thought he was going to either shoot me or die of fright, or both. I waved my passport and suitcase and when he saw the flag, his face contorted to the "Why me?" look. After taking a deep breath, he signaled for me to wait outside. He waved his arms and talked excitedly on the phone until three US Army jeeps converged from different directions. After I told them where I'd been, they put me in one of the jeeps and drove me to an Army camp somewhere in West Germany.

For the next three days I was debriefed by military intelligence specialists who asked me for everything from the film to my train ticket and hotel bill. They had great food at that camp and when they got everything I had (except the flag), they thanked me and assigned a driver to drop me off in Munich.

When I returned to New York, everything had changed. The Viet Nam war was raging and Hunter College was the scene of sit-ins and anti-war demonstrations. I didn't want to go to war, so I registered for classes, but just couldn't do it. When the Army gave me a physical they said they didn't want me. High blood pressure, the doctor said.

In 1970 I got a job as an overseas buyer and was living in Casablanca, Morocco, where I bought handicrafts for export to the states. I learned French and basic Arabic and with a local artisan started a factory making leather wallets and change purses. The Moroccans thought I was nuts, but Bloomingdale's wanted bright purple leather, so that's what we made.

Moroccan leather has an unmistakable smell which some say is caused by urine in the tanning solution. To make a long story short, I made sure the chemicals were changed often and left the tanned hides in the hot sun for a whole day so the smell was all but gone when they arrived in New York.

Business in Morocco is complicated, so each month I checked merchandise as baggage and delivered the orders myself. After visiting with clients for a few days to get more orders, I then returned to North Africa I think I made about forty trips. Unfortunately, that was before frequent flier programs.

The Pan Am nonstop between New York and Casablanca was known as The African Queen. On one arrival in New York, a classmate from high school was the US Customs Inspector and shortly after that trip I began making regular visits to the Customs Office in lower Manhattan. They wanted to know the prices of Moroccan goods, among other things.

Business was good and if the orders were finished on time, I brought gifts back for the workers and their families. It became a fun tradition to count the wallets and change purses out loud in arabic as we inspected and packed them. At the end, we all shouted the only English I ever taught them: "Out of sight!"

By far the most popular gifts were Timex watches, which cost very little in New York and were not available in Morocco. I bought them from a little shop on 14th Street where the owner, Jewel "Julie" Goldstein, a rotund Jewish business man who never frowned, always had 30 watches for me at a "special price". Unfortunately, not all of the workers got watches because an "unidentified black male in his twenties" robbed then stabbed Julie to death. The killer was never identified.

I didn't make much money, but I sure did love Casablanca. My maid, Aisha, a tiny woman with endless energy, received $5 per week. One day when I arrived home for lunch, she signaled me to remain still, then deftly grabbed a pigeon from the window sill, killed it and asked if she could take it home. When I tried to give her $20. in Moroccan dirhams for her family, she refused and said everyone would think she'd stolen it.

After a few years, life in Morocco turned me into a fatalist. I believed things happened because they were supposed to. I also believed if something wasn't supposed to occur, there wasn't much you could do about it.

When I proposed to my first and only wife, Carol, I said if there were any obstacles, maybe we should wait. When we went to the American Embassy, they laughed and said the paperwork would take forever. As we turned to leave, they smiled and told us about Gibraltar. Half an hour later we became "bachelor and spinster," residents of Gibraltar with a ceremony scheduled for the day after our arrival. Everyone wished us happiness.

The following morning there was a train leaving for Tangiers, but all flights from there to Gibraltar were booked. We looked at each other, figured it wasn't meant to happen, but decided to at least visit Tangiers. When we got there, the airline ticket agent was the brother of my banker, who smiled broadly and assigned us great seats. In Gibraltar, I had hardly any cash. Our taxi driver/philosopher said, "Don't worry! You have all of your lives ahead of you". He was right. Everybody took American Express and we've been married ever since.

In 1975, two attempts were made to assassinate King Hassan II. As civil unrest began to surface, I traveled less and when we left in December, we knew it might be for the last time. As I said, Morocco is complicated, but if you bring dollars in, you can leave with just about anything. I'd become friendly with the Customs Supervisor at Nouasser Airport in Casablanca and had been going to see him each time I left for the required export stamps on my documentation.

Each month I dropped a 100 dirham note ($20.) on the floor, picked it up and said "Hassan my friend, I just found this on the floor, is it yours?" Usually, he would thank me and put the note (back) in his pocket. On my last trip, when I asked Hassan if the note was his, he said "No, my good friend, I dropped a 500 dirham note."

On that trip my wife and I were questioned and searched separately by armed soldiers. A douanier I knew told me that my many trips had been noticed and I had been identified as a suspected CIA operative. This wasn't true, but that didn't seem to matter. We left our apartment, furniture, photos, record albums and keepsakes and never returned. We tried to donate our piano to the cultural center, but don't know if they ever got it.

In 1976, my wife and I drove a motor home west, ran out of gas in south Orange County and we've been there ever since. We like it because it's just like Morocco, with plenty of palm trees and great weather.

In September 1976 I was invited by the Department of Defense to return to Germany as a civilian reporter with the temporary rank of Major. My orders were to report on combat readiness of the combined NATO forces assembled in Germany for the Autumn Forge military exercise. It was an incredible experience traveling from one international camp to another by helicopter. It was a challenge to anyone's stomach.

After more than a dozen jarring ups and downs, I went to a building once used by Hitler's top staff members. The basement had been converted to an Officer's Club and I was in need of a beer. As I approached the bar, a friendly Irish soldier in his fifties offered to buy me a drink. I asked if he was on active duty and he replied, "I'm a chaplain. I'm hearing confessions and this is good a place as any! Anything you'll be wanting to tell me?" We had a good laugh, but I think he was quite serious. I know I heard a lot of confessions when I was a bartender.

For a month I traveled with a Thunderjet squadron of Air Force pilots from George Air Force Base in the high desert area of San Bernardino county. The seasoned pilots of those powerful F-104 jets saw a lot of action in Viet Nam. They got their names because like thunder, they came out of nowhere. They flew as low as one hundred feet off the ground through enemy territory. Instant awesome power.

When I returned to California I could hardly speak because I'd seen so much. After that experience with information overload, I understood what can happen in law enforcement. It seemed to take me forever to write that report and I honestly don't know how cops keep it together with all they see and do. It can be tough.

In 1980, after working as a free lance journalist and real estate salesman, we bought an old movie theater and a restaurant. I decided south Orange County needed a live theater for concerts, so we stopped showing movies and went into the entertainment business. After successful concerts with Chuck Berry, Jerry Lee Lewis and George Thorogood, we added Comedy Night.

A couple of new comedians we featured were Jerry Seinfeld and Bob Saget. We paid $250 for two shows and they were happy to have it. Talk about inflation. Now they get a lot more than $250 a minute!

In 1981, I was approached by a man who said he was an attorney. He said wanted to buy the business and we agreed on a deal, but he delayed and delayed until we lost ownership of the theater and he took over for no money. Later I learned that he was a disbarred attorney who'd been convicted of felony drug sales.

That was when I learned first hand the value of investigation. One simple phone call to the State Bar could have saved me from making a mistake which changed my life. The silver lining is that after that debacle, my wife suggested I become an attorney, so I went to law school and became an investigator.

We sold the restaurant at a loss and I started over at Western State School of Law in Fullerton in 1981. I worked as a student interviewer for the Orange County Public Defender as part of the work study program, but with a family to take care of, tuition became unaffordable. I transferred to night school at Pacific Coast School of Law in Long Beach.

In 1982, I began working full time as the in house investigator for a law firm with eighteen attorneys and I was busy all the time. Finding out what happened interested me more than the legal arguments, so I dropped out of law school and became a licensed private investigator.

One of my first assignments was to locate a stolen tour bus previously owned by Elvis Presley. Anaheim PD located the bus, which had been re-registered in Louisiana and sold twice. The assignment became a legal bowl of spaghetti, so I went on to other cases, but during that time I met Jim Mason.

Mason, whose laugh was as big as his belly, was one of the best auto repo guys in the business. We hit it off pretty well and I started using him to skip trace deadbeats and locate witnesses and the attorneys in the office were impressed at how I could find just about anyone. We had some victories and shared a few celebration dinners. Things went very well for about six months.

Jim always drove old cars and when he needed wheels while his was in the shop, I borrowed one for him from a client. A few days later, the client called:

"The police just called. They've got the car. Jimmie was in it. He's dead! Better go check it out." And so began my first contact with the Orange County Sheriff's Department.

I knew Jim had been hired by Municipal Court Judge Bobby Youngblood to work on his 1982 campaign for Orange County Sheriff. He told me he'd come upon some really hot information which would help Youngblood. He had it in his briefcase and wasn't going to turn it over until he saw the money, he said. I had no time to get involved. If it didn't concern one of my cases, I didn't want to know about it.

When he was found, Jim, who weighed about 350 lbs., was parked in the manager's space at a motel in Artesia. It looked like he knew he was in trouble and parked there so someone would check on him. The manager found him when he arrived at 7:00 a.m., but by then, it was too late.

Remembering what he'd said, I checked out the car and there was no briefcase. The police had been there already, so I thought maybe they had it. Couple of lottery tickets (losers), a motel key, but no briefcase. At the motel, the manager said they evicted him for non payment. Nothing was left in the room.

Jim had an ex-wife and when I called to report the bad news, she was very upset. He had promised to pay his delinquent child support with the money he was getting. She wanted me to find the briefcase because it had "explosive" information in it. She said she had no money to bury him and there was no insurance. That was certainly not the conversation I expected.

Jim told me several times that his greatest pleasure was to

shave his face as smooth as possible every day. When he died he had a three day growth of beard, so I knew his last days were not pleasant. I asked a friend at the LA Coroner's Office to check property. Jim had a business card identifying him as a consultant to the Youngblood for Sheriff campaign, but no briefcase.

I assumed that if Jim's death was in any way connected to what he had in his briefcase, the Orange County Sheriff's Department would want to know about it. The Coroner's Office agreed to run a drug screen for possible poisoning and forward the results to OCSD. I was never able to confirm whether that was done.

A huge man, Jim was only forty-two. The LA Sheriff's Department opened a homicide file, but that's routine when death is not witnessed. They had no reason to suspect foul play. I told them about the business card and the missing briefcase. They listened, then closed their file.

The following day I went to the Orange County Sheriff's Department to tell them about Jim's death and the missing briefcase. A Lieutenant seemed interested. He told me Sheriff Gates had a "special unit" of investigators for these situations and I should go back to my office and wait for a call.

I'm still waiting for that call. For a long time I had the same feeling I'd had in Morocco. You know there's something going on, but there's a piece missing and you just can't put it together.

A few months after Jim Mason died, I learned he'd been a confidential informant for the FBI. Then I found out that Jim Mason wasn't even his real name.

Rest in peace, whoever you were.

* * *

I've never been much for politics, but I became interested in the 1982 campaign for Orange County Sheriff because of Jim. I'd heard stories about Watergate-like activities which were pretty outrageous. Two investigators from the Sheriff's "special unit" covertly videotaped a lecture by Professor George Wright. An outspoken critic of Sheriff Gates who had run against him in 1978, Wright and his colleagues were justifiably outraged.

After the election was over and Brad Gates was elected for his third term, Judge Youngblood, George Wright and private investigator Pat Bland sued the Sheriff's Department and the "special unit" known as the Orange County Criminal Activity System (OCCAS). Taxpayers paid $375,000 to avoid a trial.

Soon after the case settled, I met with Professor Wright and was fascinated to hear some of the things that went on. He showed me his unfinished book. A few weeks later, he gave me his notes and entire case file and I began writing the first edition of The Twisted Badge.

In 1990, George Wright considered running again for Sheriff, but was unable to qualify because the filing requirements had been changed to allow only POST (Police Officers Standards and Training) qualified law enforcement officers to run. This change, which also excluded federal investigators and judges, was quietly introduced and adopted in the late eighties. Was this done to make sure that fewer people qualified to run against Sheriff Brad Gates? Politics and law enforcement make strange bedfellows.

After Professor Wright confirmed he could not run, we hosted a meeting at the Irvine Hilton to see if there were any qualified candidates. Nick Novick, a former DA who had run against Capizzi in 1990, introduced Don Bankhead. Recently retired from the Fullerton Police Department, Commander Bankhead was very qualified to run for Sheriff. Though I'm still not very interested in politics, I did become involved in the 1990 election and Bankhead was nearly elected after only a three month campaign.

In 1994, Bankhead, then the Mayor of Fullerton, decided not

to run again because a recall campaign had been mounted against the city council members who voted for a utility tax. The recall which kept Bankhead out of the Sheriff's race was successful, but only to a point. He was recalled effective October 18, but was then re-elected 21 days later on November 8, 1994. Since then, he has served two years as Mayor and three as Mayor Pro-Tem. Bankhead recently announced that he will run for the Assembly in the 72nd District. I've always wondered about how perfectly timed that recall was to eliminate Bankhead as a candidate.

In early 1995, Orange County DA Michael Capizzi decided to prosecute Supervisors Roger Stanton and William Steiner because they had failed to prevent the largest bankruptcy in US history. If Bill Steiner had resigned and returned to the private sector, we might never have known the lengths to which the DA was willing to go for another notch on his prosecutorial shotgun.

Supervisor Stanton became the target of an enormously expensive investigation into allegations that he knew former Orange County Tax Collector Robert Citron was making very risky investments. Stanton, whose babysitter was DA Capizzi's daughter, decided to resign and return to teaching.

Supervisor Gaddi Vasquez, a rising star in the Republican party and a former police officer, resigned early on when he was tipped off about what was about to happen. No longer conducting the business of his constituents, he now works for Southern California Edison, the company that conducts electricity for the people he once represented.

Supervisor Bill Steiner spoiled Capizzi's plan by refusing to resign and/or say anything that wasn't true. He soon realized that his informal meetings with prosecutors and investigators were being used to build a case and he hired attorney Allan Stokke. The questionable tactics used by the DA are detailed in the Bankruptcy chapter of this book.

In early 1998, Sheriff Gates' friend, confidant and onetime heir apparent, Dennis LaDucer, infamous within the department for a series of unpunished peccadillos, finally went too far. The highest ranking female in the department, Wendy Costello, tired of his incessant sexual innuendos, filed a lawsuit against him and against the Sheriff for not stopping it. When her story broke, four more female deputies came forward and for LaDucer, there was no code of silence.

Sheriff Gates probably didn't want to keep forgiving his friend, didn't want to keep giving him one more chance. Lieutenant Costello, whose husband was an investigator in the department, hired LA attorney Pat Thistle to represent her. When the DA's office predictably declined to file criminal charges, Attorney Thistle told local newspapers: "I've got a rock solid case. The filing of criminal charges would only have delayed our trial. We're ready to go!"

After an internal investigation, Gates abruptly fired LaDucer, who immediately filed a wrongful termination case against the Sheriff, the Department and the County. This was not going to be an easy case to defend because the Sheriff had failed to deal with LaDucer. He had failed to supervise his people. He had failed.

Assistant Sheriff Doug Storm had been groomed for several years to be the next Sheriff. In the tradition of Orange County politics, Gates announced his retirement and called a press conference to bless the candidacy of his chosen successor. That didn't go well either. The press conference was not well attended and many of Gates' political contributors had already endorsed Orange County Marshall Mike Carona, who was promising an audit of the department.

Doug Storm, by all accounts a nice guy, always followed orders. He'd quietly done what he was told and several of the Sheriff's friends and supporters reportedly got special treatment. Business as usual. But not in 1998. This was not a good year for Brad Gates.

The 1998 election for Orange County Sheriff was not business as usual. Brad Gates, cowboy Sheriff, decided it was time for him to ride off into the golden sunset and District Attorney Michael Capizzi made his move to be California's next Attorney General. The voters replaced them both with candidates they did not endorse and both now face uncertain futures. It was definitely not business as usual in Orange County.

Marshall Carona started early and by mid 1998, he had an impressive list of supporters. Mike Carona, with his disarmingly quiet manner, is all business when the chips are down. He and Gates battled when the Sheriff tried unsuccessfully to absorb the Marshall's Office into the Sheriff's Department. Gates called Carona unqualified and Carona responded that Gates was resistant to change. It will be very interesting to see what the twenty four year career of Brad Gates looks like on paper.

During his tenure as Sheriff, Brad Gates was named in more than 122 lawsuits. In his ten years as Marshall, Mike Carona was named in one. Several million taxpayer dollars were spent defending and settling civil rights and other lawsuits filed against Sheriff Gates. Far less money was needed to defend Carona, so his election was good news for taxpayers and bad news for defense lawyers.

When Assistant Sheriff Doug Storm decided politics was not for him, Mike Carona was the only Republican candidate. When Santa Ana Police Chief Paul Walters decided to oppose Carona, Sheriff Gates refused to endorse him, even though Gates complained publicly that Carona was not qualified for the job.

Carona was elected after a campaign reminiscent of the election of 1990. Santa Ana Police Chief Paul Walters, like Commander Don Bankhead, was highly qualified for the job, but had only a few months to campaign. The issue of qualifications arose, but both Walters and Carona are proven managers. The LA Times endorsed Walters, but hedged by saying both men were qualified.

Even though Sheriff Gates refused to endorse Chief Walters, the Association of Orange County Deputy Sheriffs (AOCDS) voted to provide funding and volunteers to help elect him. Walters, who is very well respected by law enforcement and community leaders, made a very good showing in the close race.

In a recent interview, Chief Walters stated that he often voiced his opinion when he didn't agree with something Gates wanted and this angered the Sheriff. He confirmed that he and the Sheriff never got along and he didn't expect an endorsement.

Chief Walters shared an experience he had with Gates at the Sheriff's Academy many years ago. He recalled Gates was teaching a class and a trainee questioned a comment he made about the behavior of suspects. When the trainee returned to the classroom after a break, Gates pointed his service revolver at him and dry fired to demonstrate to the class how he would behave in that circumstance. "Brad Gates always had to be right," said the Chief, shaking his head.

In a recent interview, newly elected Sheriff Mike Carona shared what happened when he became Sheriff. On January 4, 1999 at 11:49 a.m., he sat on a couch in his new office. Former Sheriff Brad Gates sat at the desk reading a newspaper. The bare walls bore no trace of the autographed photo of John Wayne and the cowboy sheriff's other mementos. Neither man spoke. At high noon, Gates folded the paper, slid it in the wastebasket, placed his well worn keys on the desk and walked out of the office. Sheriff Carona smiled and added "Before he'd left the building, the locks were being changed".

Sheriff Carona has asked the grand jury to look into several situations and they recently agreed with his proposal to conduct an audit. The projected cost ranged from $500,000 to $3 million. He opted for the $500,000 audit and feels that the report should be ready in late 1999.

Sheriff Carona was very upbeat during the interview and said he feels his first few months as Sheriff went better than expected. Relaxing in his newly decorated office, he said "There's a feeling of optimism in the department".

As we approach the millennium, I wonder what Orange County will be like without the good old boys.

* * *

2

One Free Shot

When I got the call, I knew exactly what to do. After the meeting with homicide, I knew nothing I'd done mattered.

Yvonne Grisanti Clarke (R.I.P.)

On Sunday afternoon October 28, 1990, Robert Clarke, a recently retired investigator with the California Department of Justice, shot his wife in the back of the head. A former member of a multi-jurisdictional narcotics suppression task force, he shot her as she was typing in her tiny upstairs office in their new home in San Juan Capistrano. She was dead on arrival at a local hospital.

Robert Clarke told responding deputies that he was cleaning his gun at a small table in Yvonne's office when it unexpectedly discharged. He did not tell them that he had recently settled a workers' comp stress claim and wasn't supposed to use a firearm.

About a week after the shooting, I got a phone call from Dr. Robert Bucklin, a nationally respected expert pathologist with whom I'd worked on several murder cases. Now based in Las Vegas, Dr. Bucklin, who has performed thousands of autopsies, told me that the victim, Yvonne Clarke, was his part time typist. He retained me to investigate the circumstances surrounding her death because Robert Clarke was in law enforcement and Dr. Bucklin thought the Sheriff's Department might not be unbiased.

He was right.

Dr. Bucklin sent me a copy of the autopsy report and told me that the trajectory of the bullet which entered Yvonne Clarke's head was from a point above her and she could not have been shot as described by her husband.

Robert and Yvonne Clark had a large mortgage and very high balances on all their credit cards. I called Bob and Viola Grisanti, Yvonne's parents, turned on a tape recorder and asked them to tell me all the reasons this might not have been an accidental shooting. A copy of this very emotional one hour tape was made part of my file.

Bob and Viola told me their daughter hated guns and wouldn't let her husband bring one into a room. Clarke said he was upstairs in Yvonne's office where she typed transcriptions for her clients. The Grisanti's said his gun was stored away in a downstairs closet. It was never upstairs and there was no way she would let Bob Clarke sit in her tiny office and clean a gun he wasn't supposed to carry.

The Grisanti's noted that Yvonne's reading glasses were on the bed stand. She wore them when she typed, so why wasn't she wearing them? They gave me a list of people who knew both Yvonne and her husband.

Next I called Chief Assistant District Attorney Maury Evans to let him know that I would be contacting witnesses and to ask him which homicide investigators had been assigned to the case. He called me back right away to say that the case had been assigned to Gary Bale and Tom Giffen.

I knew that if I checked in with Maury Evans, I'd be able to contact him later if a problem arose. I could always count on Maury to take and return my calls. I told him I'd provide all work product to Investigators Bale and Giffen so his office could make an informed decision on whether or not to file charges.

I left a message for Investigators Bale and Giffen, but didn't get a return call. I didn't expect one. Then I started to call the names on the list and things began to develop. The life insurance policy had already been paid to the beneficiary, Robert Clarke. I asked the life insurance company to call Investigators Giffen and Bale to confirm the amount of the policy and the date it was paid. I don't know if that ever happened.

On December 2, 1990, only thirty-five days after the shooting, Robert Clarke issued check number 104 from a Sun Life of Canada life insurance policy in the amount of $3,843 to reimburse the Grisanti family for funeral costs. He later married the woman with whom he'd been having an extramarital affair.

As soon as I found out that Robert Clarke had filed a workers' comp case against the California Department of Justice, I went to the Santa Ana Workers Compensation Appeals Board (WCAB). Very few people know these records are available. I reviewed the Clarke file and photocopied everything in it, including several psychiatric evaluations. According to these evaluations, which were filed by Clarke's attorney and the insurance company, Robert Clarke was unstable and should no longer carry a weapon.

According to the file, Clarke's case was settled for a lump sum of about $13,000 so he didn't get very much when all was said and done. At the time of the shooting, he was working as a bartender in Dana Point.

Witnesses told me Yvonne was upset because her earnings were being used to pay delinquent child support to her husband's first wife. Then I heard about the infidelities. Yvonne had been with another man at least once and Clarke had been seeing the woman he later married. I identified the parties, but didn't risk contacting them because I didn't want to hamper the criminal investigation that I hoped was taking place. I decided to maintain a low profile and make everyone deal directly with Yvonne's parents.

When I finally met with Gary Bale and Tom Giffen in late December 1990, they had their investigation file with them. It was less than an inch thick and I sensed they weren't following up on anything. I figured they weren't going to do anything with my report either, so I didn't write one. I handed them copies of the psychological evaluations and a typed list of the witnesses I'd contacted and their contact numbers. I told them what each witness had to say and that it looked to me like Robert Clarke had murdered his wife.

When Bale and Giffen saw those psych reports, they were ready to jump all over me. I had to explain to them that these kind of reports are routinely made part of workers' comp files, but they were clearly concerned that I'd been able to get them. I also gave them a copy of my taped interview with Bob and Viola Grisanti. I knew they'd have to log it in and someone might actually listen to it.

As I went through my list of what each witness would say, Bale and Giffen didn't take notes. I assumed the room was bugged and that was fine with me. This was very possibly premeditated murder for profit. A death penalty case.

I talked, they listened and after about twenty minutes I asked them if they were going to contact the extra marital partners. To my surprise, they said they already had. They said they didn't think the case should be filed because they didn't want to "sully the reputation of Yvonne by bringing up her infidelity." I was surprised by their candor, but not by what they said. I only hoped the DA wouldn't go along with them.

After the meeting, Bale and Giffen walked me to the elevator. Once we were away from the room (and the bugs) I asked them if they had copies of The Twisted Badge. They both smiled so broadly, no answer was necessary.

In May of 1991, the Grisantis received a letter from Deputy DA Bernadette Cemore stating that no charges would be filed against Robert Clarke due to lack of evidence. A subsequent request for a grand jury investigation resulted in a similar letter. A request for assistance from the FBI also went nowhere.

Robert Clarke married his mistress and moved to Mexico for a few years. They presently live in San Diego County. Deputy DA Cemore resigned from the DA's Office and now works for the public defender's office. Bob Grisanti died of cancer in 1996.

My deposition was taken in connection with a civil case filed by the Grisanti's and the son of Robert Clarke against the gun manufacturer. The attorney for the gun maker subpoenaed my file and questioned me for two sessions about everything I'd done. It looked like Robert Clarke was finally going to have to tell his story to a jury.

I was subpoenaed to testify at trial, but the case was settled. The attorney for the gun maker told me he could not discuss it, but a family member told me that the gun maker paid about $15,000, which was less than the cost of a trial.

In March 1999, I met with newly elected Sheriff Mike Carona and gave him a copy of this chapter. He agreed to review the investigation file in an effort to determine whether Robert Clarke was given one free shot. Sheriff Carona said he would discuss the case with newly elected District Attorney Tony Rackauckas and he suggested I contact the DA in a few weeks.

In April 1999 I met with District Attorney Rackauckas and he confirmed that the shooting death of Yvonne Clarke had been investigated by the DA's Office. He told me he wanted to have a another look at it and he'd assigned Assistant District Attorney Mike Jacobs to review the file.

Jacobs, head of the homicide panel, recently spearheaded a campaign to use modern technology and DNA evidence to clear unsolved crimes. One of the cases Jacobs reviewed involved former Marine Kevin Green, who had been convicted of rape and assault. Green had already served many years in prison, but DNA evidence cleared him and Jacobs expedited his release. The actual rapist, Gerald Parker, is now in prison.

Did Robert Clarke get one free shot? Mike Jacobs has a lot of cases, but I'm sure he'll get to this one.

* * *

Darryn Robins (R.I.P.)

Darryn Robins loved being a cop. The best part of his job, he said, was going to elementary and intermediate schools to talk to youngsters about staying away from drugs. As a black man in a predominantly white county, Robins made an impression on the kids. He liked them and they liked him.

Robins pulled duty on Christmas day in 1993. He didn't know when he left his home in Los Angeles that he would never return to his wife and one year old daughter, Melissa, whom he lovingly called his "bag of diamonds." No one could have imagined that Darryn Robins would be shot in the face that day by a gun that wasn't supposed to be loaded.

Brian Scanlan somehow became a training officer even though he had "anger management problems" and the county had already quietly paid money to citizens who threatened to sue.

Officer Robins died because Scanlan violated a cardinal rule and used a loaded gun during an "impromptu" training exercise. There were no witnesses. The video camera in Robins' unit was on, but for some reason, the shooting itself wasn't available to investigators. Obviously a malfunction, a Sheriff's Department spokesman announced.

Sheriff Gates managed to keep critical details of what happened out of the press, but the bottom line is that Scanlan should not have been a training officer. While Sheriff Gates may not have personally promoted Scanlan, he could have reversed the action because he knew of Scanlan's anger management problems. He knew the County had paid claims based on citizen complaints.

Sheriff Gates lobbied the Board of Supervisors to pay almost $2 million to the Robins family. The Board decided that Robins' death was work related and should be handled under the workers' comp program. There remains some question as to whether or not they were provided with all of the information.

Sheriff Gates was involved in this situation from the afternoon it happened until "a few top county officials" agreed to pay $10,000,000 to Officer Robins' family.

On December 5, 1995, almost two years after the shooting, the *LA Times* printed a story which questioned why Deputy Scanlan was not charged. This article is quoted verbatim as follows:

SETTLEMENT:
Secret deal involved case of officer shot in training exercise two years ago, in which no charges were ever filed.
Bankruptcy Court must OK proposal.
By
Davan Maharaj and Matt Lait, Times Staff Writers

"In a case in which Orange County grand jurors and federal prosecutors found no wrongdoing, a few top county officials secretly made a deal to pay $10 million to the family of a sheriff's deputy slain by a fellow officer during an impromptu training exercise on Christmas Day two years ago.

County sources said the offer to survivors of Deputy Darryn Leroy Robins was strongly pushed by Sheriff Brad Gates, who wanted to compensate the family and avoid an embarrassing legal battle involving his department.

The proposed settlement was reached last March, the same month in which bankrupt Orange County decided to lay off hundreds of county employees because of its dire financial situation.

The deal, which could become one of the largest settlements in county history, still needs final approval from the U.S. Bankruptcy Court and a committee of top county officials.

Terms of the settlement with Robins' wife, his 3-year-old daughter and his mother were disclosed in documents recorded in

Bankruptcy Court along with a flood of other last-minute claims filed before last Friday's deadline.

Both the victim's family and county officials were eager to settle the matter out of court. Without a lawsuit ever being filed, the parties even agreed to take their dispute to a private mediation firm in Orange to broker a settlement agreement.

Tom Beckett, the county's risk manager, said he and Dennis Bunker, county claims manager, authorized a Newport Beach financial firm to try to settle the case for $10 million after reviewing the county's liability. Beckett said the settlement would need final approval by a claim settlement committee comprising Chief Executive Officer, County Counsel Laurence M. Watson and Auditor-Controller Steve Lewis. The Board of Supervisors, which years ago delegated authority to settle claims to the three-member committee, would not need to approve the agreement, officials said.

At least one supervisor was surprised at the settlement offer. "I thought all this stuff got tied up in the bankruptcy and was put on hold," Supervisor William G. Steiner said.

Thomas A. Girardi, a Los Angeles attorney who represents Robins' relatives, said the officer's widow "wanted desperately to settle this case."

"The courtroom was not her first choice," Girardi said. "She did not want to go through the emotional toll that a trial like this would take on her family."

Although Officer Brian P. Scanlan steadfastly maintained that he accidentally fired the shot that killed his 38-year-old partner, the incident rocked the Sheriff's Department and shocked the community. The shooting sparked allegations of gross misconduct and racism. District attorney's office investigators maintained that the shooting was not intentional but a tragic accident.

Authorities said the two deputies were engaged in an unscheduled training exercise behind a Lake Forest movie theater, with Robins playing the part of a suspect in a car stop and Scanlan the arresting officer, when the shooting occurred.

Scanlan, a 32-year-old field training deputy, told investigators that he shot Robins accidentally after Robins startled him by pulling a hidden handgun from behind the visor of his patrol car.

Robins, authorities said, was apparently imitating a technique used by gang members against police.

The Orange County district attorney's office concluded after an investigation that Scanlan had been "grossly negligent" in using a loaded pistol in a training exercise, and thought he should be charged with involuntary manslaughter.

But in an unusual twist, prosecutors left the final decision to the grand jury, which declined to indict Scanlan. Critics of the county's investigation questioned whether the case was handled properly, and whether the shooting was ascribable to a "trigger-happy" cop. They also questioned whether the shooting had anything to do with the slain officer being African American and the shooter being white.

At the urging of the victim's family and community leaders, Justice Department officials looked into the case but said they found no violations of federal law.

Scanlan has since been granted a service-connected disability retirement in which he receives about $2,100. per month. He now lives in Rio Rico, Arizona, where he works as a private investigator. In August 1994, Robins' widow, Rosemary, filed a claim with the county on behalf of herself and daughter Melissa, aged 3. She alleged that deputies were holding training sessions with loaded weapons in violation of department policy.

After the shooting, Sheriff Gates expressed deep concern for Mrs. Robins, and visited her at her home in Los Angeles several times. According to a county official close to the settlement talks, Gates "wanted to get the case settled before a claim was even filed."

The official added that at one point, the sheriff tried to get the county to buy Robins' widow a house as part of an eventual settlement. Gates wielded considerable influence in the county earlier this year when he became a key member of the county's bankruptcy recovery team. Gates did not return calls seeking comment Monday.

The family's attorney and county officials confirmed Monday that the proposed settlement has been in the works for months. The deal was brokered through Judicial Arbitration & Mediation Services, Inc. which for a fee helps settle civil disputes and avoid long court battles.

Under the proposed deal, the widow would receive a lump sum payment of $1.1 million with the rest of her settlement to be paid over a 20-year period. The deputy's daughter would receive $50,000 a year at ages 18 through 21 for education costs. She would get a $100,000 lump sum at age 25, according to the deal. Robins' mother, Mildred Fisher, would get payments starting at $300 per month for the next 10 years.

James Brady, a vice president of Ringler Associates, a Newport Beach firm that crafted the settlement for the county, said the deal was held up because the county needed Bankruptcy Court approval to purchase annuities to fund the payments.

Settlement talks between Robins' attorney and the county occurred at a time when many civil lawsuits against the county have been stuck in legal purgatory. After the county declared insolvency, federal bankruptcy law automatically froze all pending cases against the county until the bankruptcy is resolved.

The Robins case is unusual because it was tentatively settled after the family filed a claim but before the filing of a formal lawsuit.

Girardi, Robins' attorney, praised the sheriff for his "upstanding" manner in dealing with his client's claim. "He dealt with the matter with a great deal of integrity," Girardi said.

Girardi, however, said he is concerned about the county's bankruptcy and its impact on the settlement. He plans to raise the issue before the private mediator next month.

"We are hopeful that the county will do the right thing and not oppose the settlement.," Girardi said.

(Ken Ellingwood and Michael G. Wagner contributed to this report.)

END OF ARTICLE

The Robins shooting was determined to be the result of "gross negligence" by Deputy Scanlan. According to the *LA Times*, the district attorneys who reviewed the case recommended that Scanlan be charged with involuntary manslaughter. Why were the attorneys charged with the decision to file or not file against Scanlan ignored? Was the grand jury given the whole story? Why was 32-year-old Brian Scanlan given one free shot, then rewarded with $2,100. per month for the rest of his life?

Instead of moving Brian Scanlan out, Sheriff Gates moved him up, then rewarded him after he violated the single most important rule for training officers. Instead of moving Dennis LaDucer out, Sheriff Gates moved him up.

These management decisions have cost taxpayers a lot of money. Sheriff Gates may be retired, but he will still have to answer for what happened on his watch.

In April 1999 I met with District Attorney Tony Rackauckas, who said he had reviewed the law. He explained that while there appears to have been a basis to file involuntary manslaughter charges against Scanlan, manslaughter is not murder and there *is* a statute of limitations.

DA Tony Rackauckas concluded that the filing deadline had passed and no charges could be filed. Did Brian Scanlan get one free shot? I think he did. And he got paid for it.

* * *

One Free Shot

3

Black and Blue

The beating of Rodney King by LAPD Officers was a defining moment in our history. At the writing of this edition, President Clinton has been impeached, but not removed from office. Reverend Jerry Falwell is quoting Rodney King, not Martin Luther King: "Can't we all just get along?"

Unbelievable as it seemed, in 1991 the United States was at war and a new cable network, CNN, was airing footage of tanks and bombings as if they were reporting on the mother of all drive by shootings. I was glued to the TV as I watched military operations play out on international television, followed by military command briefings. CNN's Christiane Amanpour and Bernard Shaw told us what was happening amid tracer fire and sirens. That was the year the super bowl became a patriotic statement.

As Patriot missiles shot down scuds, the people of Israel prepared for chemical warfare. Gas masks were provided to everyone, including trembling news reporters. Tourism in that part of the world became history.

In a matter of days, the war was over and most Americans returned to their regularly scheduled programs. By then, CNN had become a major factor in world news gathering. I still check CNN Headline News to make sure I'm not missing anything.

In the early morning hours of March 3, 1991, Rodney King and his longtime friends, Freddie Helms and Bryant "Poo" Allen, were driving along gently rolling hills on the deserted 210 freeway west of Pasadena . They'd had a few beers and were feeling mellow as they drove along listening to a tape on the car radio. Suddenly, a CHP patrol unit bathed the small Hyundai in white and flashing lights.

King froze. If he pulled over, they'd smell beer. He'd just served 13 months on a two year sentence in state prison for a robbery conviction. His parole would be violated and he'd be sent back for 11 more months.

As he thought things through, King decided to exit at Osborne and drive to Lakeview Terrace. Careful not to speed, he drove until he decided what to do. He thought his best bet would be to stop at a well lit spot where there might be people around to watch three black men in a Hyundai get pulled over. He knew only too well that police officers don't like to be ignored.

King used to fish with his father at nearby Hansen Dam and he remembered a popular drive-in on Foothill Avenue that stayed open late. More bad luck. He almost missed the place because it had gone out of business and was dark.

He found a working street light, pulled over and waited. CHP Officer Melanie Singer approached the car and instructed him to put his hands where she could see them. King complied, but when Singer ordered him to exit the vehicle he was jerked back by the seat belt he forgot he was wearing. That's when all hell broke loose.

Amid the commotion of LAPD units, a helicopter and a Los Angeles Unified School District patrol unit with its siren left blaring, King got out of the car and complied with shouted instructions. He laid on his stomach on the cold ground and the beating began. Beaten, hit with taser darts, then hog tied, he was dragged on gravel to wait for an ambulance. Freddie Helms, who'd been asleep, and Bryant Allen, were handcuffed, but not arrested. They were left there to walk home when the car, which belonged to King's mother, was impounded.

After high fives were exchanged by several officers and a felony report for evading arrest had been prepared, George Holliday, a resident of the apartment complex across the street, called the LAPD Foothill Division.

Holliday explained that he had videotaped the beating of a black man from his apartment balcony with his new camcorder because he sensed this was not a routine matter. When LAPD expressed no interest, he called Channel 5 News. They bought the tape for $500 and ran it on the evening news. The next morning, CNN ran the video worldwide, feeding tens of millions of viewers more scenes of war. A new media frenzy began and overnight, Rodney King's battered face reminded us all that the struggle between law enforcement and people of color was far from over.

The beating did not need to be analyzed. There was no need for hours of strategy discussions about how he could have prevented it. He should have pulled over. Simple as that. Was the beating justified? Had LAPD officers been caught in the act of taking out all their personal and professional frustrations on this one black man? Was President Kennedy killed by a lone gunman?

Arthur Oviedo (R.I.P.)

To me, the King beating was especially troubling. Several years earlier I'd been hired by the family of a 24-year-old Hispanic inmate who was killed in the Orange County Jail.

Arthur Oviedo lived with his mother and two sisters in a small house in southern LA County. He steered clear of trouble as a teenager and was working in Fullerton when trouble found him.

An avid body builder, Oviedo worked out every day after working in a warehouse in Fullerton. In his enthusiasm to achieve perfect muscle tone, he started injecting illegal steroids. One day as he was walking to the gym, a Fullerton police officer stopped him to ask where he was going. Oviedo had a syringe tucked in his weight glove and, like King, he panicked and didn't stop.

The officer chased him, shot him 3 times with a taser, arrested him for assault on a police officer and transported him to Orange County Jail. His inmate jacket identified him as having assaulted an officer and that same night he was beaten in the toilet area (where there are no video cameras) by "unidentified" persons. Injured, he was moved to the infirmary, where he was given haldol, a controversial psycho tropic drug which keeps problem patients in a zombie state.

Why was Arthur Oviedo, who had no prior criminal record, stopped by an officer while walking on a public street? It soon became clear that if Oviedo had not run, he would be alive.

I obtained the Oviedo family's written consent in order to access the medical records from the jail. According to his chart, Arthur Oviedo was given lithium in addition to haldol the morning he was taken to court. That morning he pled guilty to assaulting the officer and I questioned whether he knew what he was doing.

Santa Ana criminal defense attorney Robison Harley reviewed the case and agreed with my assessment. He filed a motion to withdraw the guilty plea, even though the defendant was dead. The motion was granted because after attorney Harley presented proof that Oviedo was under the influence of behavior controlling drugs when he entered his plea. The charges were not re-filed.

Several months later, Jerry Pick, Oviedo's cellmate in the medical facility, admitted beating Oviedo and strangling him with a shoelace. Pick was also charged with killing a previous cellmate whose death had been identified as due to natural causes. The pathologist failed to notice several broken ribs at autopsy.

Represented by court appointed attorney Milton Grimes, Jerry Pick pled insanity and the court referred him to a psychiatric facility. Hopefully, he has his own room.

The civil case filed by the Oviedo family was settled for $300,000. I believe that's the largest settlement ever paid by the County of Orange in a jail death. The family of the 72 year old inmate received $150,000. No information was ever obtained regarding the beating which placed Oviedo in the infirmary in the first place.

Joe Eaves (R.I.P.)

Another reason the Rodney King beating troubled me was the Joe Eaves case. Joe was a nice enough guy, but he had a drinking problem. One day he called 911 to report that his neighbor in Dana Point was dealing drugs, but responding deputies found no evidence. Joe kept calling 911 until finally he was arrested himself and transported to the Orange County Jail.

While he was in custody, Joe apparently said a wrong word and reportedly was "blind sided" by a deputy. After his release, he was treated for pretty serious face wounds, so it is fair to say something happened. Joe retained an attorney and alleged in a lawsuit that after he was beaten, he was forced to strip to his shorts and walk around that way.

When I was asked to take a look at the case, the first thing I did was ask for copies of the jail videos, which would either prove or disprove his claim. The video clearly showed Joe Eaves stripped to his underwear, the subject of ridicule. The jail video cameras take one picture per second, so it was a little disjointed.

Fox News had done a couple of stories about the Oviedo case, so I asked them if they would have a look at this tape to see if it could be enhanced. Nothing happened for a few weeks, so I more or less forgot about it.

Then Fox TV reporter Chris Harris called to say the tape had been placed in the wrong slot and he'd just found it. He told me the station had sent the tape out for whatever enhancement could be done. Within a week he was on the air three or four days in a row with the story of what happened to one inmate at the Orange County Jail. TV viewers got a chance to see Joe Eaves in his boxer shorts get taunted by Orange County Jail deputies.

The story would have a better ending if Joe had decided to stop drinking, but he didn't. The body of Joe Eaves was found about a year later in the Arizona desert, where he'd been beaten, robbed and murdered.

The King Team

Former LAPD Officer/private investigator Tom Owens and I had worked together a few times. He'd been a street cop for many years and knew how the system worked. Most important though, he seemed to have contacts everywhere he needed them. Tom had arrested his share of blacks and recalled that after the Watts riots in the Sixties, the LAPD decided it was important to control, control and control minorities. Police Chief Darryl Gates built a para military organization in LA and he handled problems with shows of force. Battering rams and secret units were absolutely necessary if the public was to be protected. Images of mean Mongolian invaders came to mind whenever I saw a TV news story about that battering ram.

A few days after the beating, Tom went to attorney Steve Lehrman's Beverly Hills office and literally forced his way in. A savvy personal injury attorney, Lehrman had just been hired by King and his office was a madhouse. Steve told me that his first impression was that Owens had just arrived from central casting. Tom Owens is all cop, from the walk to the talk to the attitude. He told Lehrman why the case needed an ex-LAPD street cop and was hired on the spot.

Tom Owens was the perfect investigator for Rodney King. We referred to him as King's "get out of jail free" card. Every time King got named as a suspect or arrested for something, Tom would race to the police station and then explain to King's parole officer why the allegation was bogus. Keeping King out of jail was very important to Lehrman, of course, because arrests don't help the credibility of the victim. The police know that too, and they wanted King to look bad, very bad.

When Tom asked me to get involved, I was interested in what was going on in this high profile case. Tom needed people he could trust to guard King at the hospital because there had been a number of death threats. I don't do that type of work and I was pretty busy, so I asked him to give me a call if he needed help of a different kind. Before long he did.

The first thing I did for "The King Team" was sweep their telephones for listening devices. Almost immediately I found one on Lehrman's home telephone, but not on King's. After a few curses, Lehrman recalled that a truck had been parked outside his home working on the phones. I explained the way things are in today's world of electronic everything and suggested he confine his important discussions to personal meetings with a radio on in the background. I told him to stop using his portable phone because they contain mini radio transmitters.

The next time Tom called, he needed help with background information on the officers involved in the beating. I gathered quite a bit of information and sent it to Lehrman. Public record background searches provide the leads needed to find out about a person. Divorce, bankruptcy and civil disputes often lead to documents that make good evidence. Talking to people who don't like a particular person can lead to good information, but it can also waste a lot of time. Documents are the best evidence and that's what I got for Lehrman.

No Back Door For Rodney King

The next time Tom called it was 2:00 a.m. Rodney King had been arrested by a CHP Officer for driving drunk in the parking lot at a Denny's in Orange.

He needed help getting King out of the Orange County Jail and over to the scene so we could investigate what happened. After reminding Tom that I wanted to remain low profile, I drove to the jail hoping to pick up King and get over to Denny's so he could point out where things happened. The Sheriff's Department had a different idea.

King was released at about 7:30 a.m., after every TV camera in the area had been given time to set up for the morning news. I spoke with the Watch Commander to ask if we could use a back door, but he just smiled and said "Sorry, we don't have a back door for Rodney King.".

That was the end of my low profile involvement with the King case. My picture was on national television and the front page of several national newspapers as Tom Owens and I guided King to my car. As Tom cursed at them to get out of the way, I was trying not to trip over the cables. The cameramen honored my request and didn't show my license plate on TV.

When we got to my car, I wasn't sure it would start. I'd been having problems with the starter and it was becoming less dependable all the time. After we got in, reporters and cameras had us surrounded. When I turned the key nothing happened. I looked at King and he just leaned back and closed his eyes. My mind was racing as I looked down at the gear shift and noticed that in my haste to park I'd left the car in drive. Slamming the shifter into park, I turned the key again. It started.

During our circuitous route to Denny's, King was tired and depressed. A big, strong man, he knew It was open season on Rodney King. He'd been arrested several times since the beating, but Tom Owens managed to keep him out of jail.King was fast becoming one of the most recognizable people anywhere.

We drove around the parking lot and King pointed out where he was parked and where he was arrested. Just as we were leaving, several TV news crews arrived, but no one saw us drive to a nearby residence hotel where he and his wife were staying. In tape recorded interviews, they described what happened.

Cristal had driven to Denny's to pick up hamburgers. While King waited in the car, she went in to get the food and even though it wasn't very crowded, it took a long time. King decided to move the car to a parking spot closer to the entrance. He pulled out, drove around the building and backed into a spot right outside the front door. Suddenly, a CHP officer was shining a light on him and ordering him out of the car.

The officer recognized King immediately, though how and when he first saw him was unclear. The police log showed that the plate had been run a few minutes before he was approached. We felt that King was under surveillance 24 hours a day, but there was no way to be sure.

King said Steve Lehrman told him emphatically not to allow any officer to take his blood or any kind of samples. For this reason, King refused to take a sobriety test and the officer placed him under arrest. King followed Lehrman's directive because he knew samples have been known to get switched.

King described one particular white officer who stood directly in front of him pounding his baton methodically into his open hand. The message was clear. Just give him a reason, any reason.

Tom Owens tracked down a lot of witnesses and Santa Ana criminal defense attorney Robison Harley took the unusual step of sharing this information with the DA's office. He told them King had not been drinking, was on private property the entire time and had violated no law.

After a thorough review, the DA's office decided not to file charges, but that wasn't the end of it. Because King had refused to take the field sobriety test (FST), his driving privileges were automatically revoked for six months.

As we prepared for the DMV hearing, I looked into the felony conviction that sent King to prison. According to King, he went to a local market to buy cigarettes and orange juice. The Korean owner would not accept food stamps, which was all he had. Upset, King threw down the food stamps and pulled over a wire stand of potato chips as he left.

According to the Korean store owner, King waited at the check stand until the register was open, then reached over and grabbed a handful of cash. As he was leaving, King threw the potato chip stand at him. The owner chased him into the street and was able to write down the license number of King's car. When the police contacted King and looked in the trunk of the car, they found cash and arrested him.

After the first day of the the DMV hearing, Tom and I were at my office when the phone rang. It was an LA Times reporter who said that Rodney King had fired Steve Lehrman and hired criminal defense attorney Milton Grimes. A multi million dollar settlement which Lehrman had worked out was not approved by the LA Board of Supervisors and apparently, King decided it would be better to have a black lawyer at trial. Even though he'd paid over $250,000 in costs up to that point, Lehrman was out.

Attorney Robison Harley handled the DMV appeal in Costa Mesa, at which we all testified. I stayed with King and his wife, Cristal,, while Grimes arrived in a Mercedes convertible and held press conferences in the parking lot. Tom kept asking Grimes if we were going to get paid and Grimes said, "Keep doing what you're doing." So we worked until the hearing was over.

DMV reversed themselves and allowed King to keep his license, but that was the last time he had Tom Owens' help. We never got paid and King seen the inside of a jail more than once.

During the trial, Americans learned the benefit of video as evidence. The jury awarded King $1.7 million, but there wasn't nearly enough money to pay all the costs involved in the case.

After the trial, Steve Lehrman was re-hired by King and structured the jury award so that his high profile client gets a substantial monthly income.

Rodney King, who is no longer on parole, started a rap music recording company. I wish him well.

* * *

Black and Blue

4

The Bankruptcy

Prior to November, 1994, Orange County Treasurer Robert Citron, legendary at earning money for Orange County cities and investors, had a situation. For years he'd been making too much money. According to sworn testimony, his staff had been skimming excess profits from some accounts. For awhile he had more money than he knew what to do with. But only for awhile.

Merrill Lynch's top salesman, Michael Stamenson, explained to Citron that the time was perfect for investments keyed to interest rates. People in the know were quietly earning millions, he said. So for millions in commissions, Merrill Lynch began selling risky investments to the pool of funds controlled by Citron, who'd been lucky, but was not a sophisticated investor. Citron knew he was taking a risk, but he had confidence in Merrill Lynch. It was their little secret.

In May 1994, Standard and Poors rated the County Pension Obligation Bond offering (with the county pool as collateral) as high as it could. At that time, they reportedly knew Citron's portfolio was almost $1 billion in the red.

In the election of 1994, the ever popular Citron had more than token opposition when accountant John Moorlach announced his candidacy. Moorlach had a copy of a portfolio analysis prepared by securities consultant Chris Street and, unlike everyone else, he understood it. He tried to debate the high risks repeatedly, but because Standard & Poors rated Citron's investments highly in May of 1994, voters (and the media) weren't inclined to listen. A few months later, everyone wished they had. When Citron pled guilty, John Moorlach was sworn in as the new Orange County Treasurer. Clearly, it pays to do your homework.

Merrill Lynch had sold Citron hundreds of millions in risky investments, but when Citron resigned on Sunday morning, December 4, 1994, all hope of a Wall Street workout vanished. The bankruptcy option was presented by attorneys and filed on the advice of attorneys who later reaped windfall earnings.

A disaster for some, the bankruptcy also provided a golden opportunity for advancement and political pay backs. The District Attorney filed criminal charges against Robert Citron, his subordinate Matthew Raabe and County Budget Director Ron Rubino. The DA then opened a grand jury investigation into the involvement of Merrill Lynch and filed charges against two supervisors for "Willful Misconduct in Office" for failing to predict or prevent it.

Citron pled guilty to felony charges of mishandling public funds. He served eight months working as a clerk in the Sheriff's Department. Citron worked off the losses he admitted he caused at the rate of $600,000 per day! Nice work if you can get it.

Former County Budget Director Ron Rubino pled guilty to a misdemeanor after his trial ended in a hung jury that voted 9 to 3 for acquittal. He served 100 hours of community service. Former Assistant Treasurer Matthew Raabe was sentenced to three years in state prison. His case is on appeal at the present time. No one was charged with doing anything for personal gain.

When the Board of Supervisors was notified about the shortfall in the investment pool, they met in frantic sessions for days without coming to a decision as to what to do. Bankruptcy lawyer Bruce Bennett explained that in bankruptcy, there would be no "run on the bank." The physically and emotionally exhausted Board of Supervisors approved the plan.

After the bankruptcy was filed, brokers who held securities as collateral sold everything. So much for the protections of bankruptcy. Sheriff Gates, District Attorney Capizzi and Health Care Agency Director Tom Uram took control of the day to day operations of the county.

Gates set his sights on several adversaries, Capizzi had his stepping stone to the Office of Attorney General and Tom Uram asked to have his offices swept for bugs.

How it All Began

As Easter pageants and spring breaks ended, April 1994 ushered in political campaign activities. John Moorlach, an accountant and candidate for County Treasurer, questioned the investment practices of Robert Citron. While many people read the headlines, few read the stories. Supervisor Bill Steiner read every one with interest and in April 1994 he asked Eileen Walsh for help. Walsh had been with the county for sixteen years and had been the Director of Finance since 1989.

Eileen Walsh talked candidly about what went on before and during the bankruptcy. Under the terms of her recently settled wrongful termination lawsuit against the county, she agreed no to talk to the press. However, the following conversations took place prior to the settlement:

MADIGAN: I understand you drafted a letter to Citron before the bankruptcy, but it was never sent?

WALSH: In April of 1994 during the Moorlach vs. Citron campaign, Supervisor Steiner asked me if there was any merit to the claims being made by Moorlach about the risky nature of

Citron's investments. He wanted to know if the claims were political rhetoric or if they had substance. I told him there were a lot of questions that needed answers, but nobody in county government wanted me to ask them. Steiner asked me to draft a letter to Citron with my questions so he could send it. I prepared the draft and delivered it to Steiner with a copy to Ernie Schneider. That afternoon Ernie came to my office and told me not to put that kind of thing in writing because if the press got it, they would make us all look bad.

MADIGAN: So what happened?

WALSH: The letter was never sent. A few weeks later, Steiner thanked me for writing it, but said he decided not to send it.

MADIGAN: Was that the end of it?

WALSH: Citron never saw the letter. He was never held accountable by the Board of Supervisors.

MADIGAN: What happened next?

WALSH: On Sunday, December 4, 1994, I was at a meeting with a large number of county officials and Matt Raabe disclosed that the treasurer's office had been skimming money from cities and schools. He said somewhere between $60 and $90 million had been taken. I suggested we contact outside law enforcement because at that time I didn't trust Sheriff Gates. In my view, the Sheriff was motivated to find as much money as possible and he was ignoring the fact that certain money was probably stolen. He never saw a tax dollar he didn't want to spend.

MADIGAN: So who did you contact?

WALSH: Nobody thought we should report the theft, so the next day I reported it to Mike Capizzi and Maury Evans. They told me they wouldn't talk to me unless I got a lawyer. I'd been asked by County Counsel Terry Andrus to hire attorneys for everyone, so I hired the law firm of Squires, Sanders & Dempsey to represent me. I hadn't slept for two days. On Tuesday, December 6, the bankruptcy was filed, then the following day DA Investigator Larry Lambert came to my office with a subpoena for my personal records.

MADIGAN: Your personal records?

WALSH: Yes, my personal papers. County employees were suspects and were treated like criminals while the supervisors and Sheriff met privately.

In early January of 1995, my attorneys met with District Attorney Capizzi, Maury Evans, Jan Nolan, Wally Wade and Guy Ormes. After a few hours, my attorneys came out and said they couldn't believe the DA wasn't at all interested in the stolen money. The DA wanted information on kickbacks to board members, known as 'pay for play' and information about Leifer Capital, financial advisors to Citron.

MADIGAN: What happened after the meeting?

WALSH: On January 19, 1995, Ernie Schneider was fired and on January 20, Tom Uram placed me on administrative leave. At 5:00 p.m. he came to my office and told me to leave and take no papers except baby pictures from my desk. Then he had police officers supervise as I was escorted from the building. That same night Sheriff Gates moved into my office with a paper shredder.

On January 21, I received a subpoena from the SEC for my personal records that were in my office. When I called to ask for access to them I was told that I would have to pay $1.15 per page for copies. On January 22, the Board of Supervisors voted not to pay my legal fees, which were about $40,000 at that time. On February 10, I received a letter transferring me to the county dump with a $30,000 pay cut.

MADIGAN: But what about the skimmed money?

WALSH: I couldn't believe it. I didn't do anything wrong and they didn't care about the crime. During that time I had hours and hours of meetings with Assistant DA Wally Wade and investigators Rusty Hodges, Mike Majors and Ken Jones. By then I was represented by LA criminal attorney Janet Levine. At the end of February 1995 I got a letter from the DA saying I was no longer a target.

MADIGAN: Was that the end of it?

WALSH: No. The DA asked to tape record my phone calls and in my suicidal state, I agreed. They asked me to make specific calls to Roger Stanton and other county officials, which they recorded. They wanted me to verify with Stanton that certain things had happened and all I wanted to do was clear my name. By early February it was clear that the DA wanted to get Roger Stanton. They wanted to know anything awful that anyone knew.

The Sheriff wanted to get Ron Rubino. He called me at home on several occasions to ask if Rubino was involved. I told him I didn't think so. I was an emotional wreck.

In late January, my secretary called to tell me that someone was downloading files from my computer. I called Maury Evans to ask if it was the DA's office and he said it wasn't them. He had the FBI inspect the computer and they verified that someone scrubbed my hard drive and there was nothing left.

END OF INTERVIEW

Walsh, who is presently working on her doctoral dissertation in Sociology at USC, teaches Sociology courses at California Polytechnic University in Pomona.

A View from the Top

In a recent interview, former Chief Administrator Ernie Schneider recalled that after the bankruptcy was filed, he received a telephone call from a trusted friend who was a judge. The friend told him to get an attorney because "Capizzi is coming after everyone.". He immediately retained a past President of the Orange County Bar Association. Schneider, who has always been known as the "go to guy" in times of trouble found himself in a difficult situation, which he described as follows:

"It was Brad's opportunity to get me out of there. He wanted to build a national narcotics training facility at Rancho Del Rio and I recommended to the Board that they sell the property. He wanted raises for his executive management people and I didn't think they were justified. The bankruptcy was his golden opportunity to get rid of me."

When asked how his termination was handled, Schneider stated:

"They had an executive session, then they called me in and said, 'We're not going to fire you, we're going to relieve you of your position.' They said they knew the bankruptcy was not my fault and I was supposed to get another assignment. Then they asked me to resign and I refused. I told them that the only person who resigned was Bob Citron and I refused to be associated with him. I let them know that if they wanted me out they'd have to fire me. After 25 years with the County, they gave me 6 months severance pay and that was it."

When asked who was to blame for the largest bankruptcy in US history, Schneider stated:

"As far as I'm concerned, I blame Citron and Merrill Lynch. They covered themselves, but they only told Citron about the risk."

When asked who the victims were, Schneider said:

"I think all the Board members and innocent county staff who lost their jobs were victims in this thing. Supervisor Gaddi Vasquez resigned because he didn't want to get indicted."

The Investigation

During the grand jury investigation into the bankruptcy, District Attorney Capizzi called a press conference to announce that his office had negotiated an agreement with Merrill Lynch. In exchange for a $30 million payment, the investigation into the actions of Merrill Lynch would be closed. Several knowledgeable attorneys have indicated that the District Attorney cannot unilaterally end a criminal investigation in exchange for money. The DA can settle cases after they've been filed, but ending a criminal investigation for a money payment may have been illegal. When asked about how this came about, Ernie Schneider stated:

"I think Capizzi was worried that if there was a trial, some stuff would come out that would make him look bad. It makes no sense that they would let Merrill Lynch off and then go after the county people with a vengeance. I was told that the guy from Merrill

Lynch had authorization for $60 million."

When asked why he felt the DA's office indicted the Board members, Schneider said:

"I think Capizzi went after the Board to deflect criticism of his office."

The transcript of the grand jury hearing at which the District Attorney decided to accept $30 million from Merrill Lynch was ordered released to the public by Superior Court Judge David Carter. The District Attorney's office filed an appeal and the transcript remains sealed.

The reason Merrill Lynch was able to buy their way off the hook may never be known because the California Supreme Court recently ruled that the DA does not have to release the transcript.

On January 3, 1999, the day before newly elected District Attorney Tony Rackauckas was sworn in, the Orange County Register ran a front page story under the headline "Capizzi heading into political oblivion." In this article, William Mitchell, the former Chairman for Orange County Common Cause, a watchdog group, stated:

"He didn't play favorites and, of course, that got him into trouble. He made a reputation for taking on political corruption. Maybe he was looking too hard to find it. When you're a hammer, all you see is nails."

This quote may help explain the series of events which took place after the bankruptcy was filed. There is some question about a possible conflict of interest because employees of the district attorney's office were investors and lost money. However, Michael Capizzi had spent his career prosecuting political corruption and he may have seen this as the case he'd been waiting for his whole life. If he did, he was wrong.

In my opinion, the decision to commence a grand jury investigation victimized many good people, Republicans and

Democrats alike.

Brad Gates and Michael Capizzi both endorsed Bill Steiner in the 1994 election. Within a matter of months, they would target Supervisor Roger Stanton and try to pressure Steiner to 'do the right thing' and help them "Get Stanton."

If they thought Supervisor Steiner was an expendable political neophyte, they were wrong.

Reflections of a Supervisor

In a recent interview, former Supervisor Bill Steiner, who served out his term and left the state, provided the following surprisingly candid details about what happened to him:

MADIGAN: Do you have any information about why Sheriff Gates and District Attorney Capizzi seemed to want to 'Get Stanton.'

STEINER: After the bankruptcy, Gates, Capizzi and Tom Uram formed a troika and they basically stepped into the vacuum left by the CAO's office, Ernie Schneider, and sort of seized power in the county. There were some jealousies and some hard feeling over that sort of... coup.

I do think that because of Roger Stanton's style, he made a lot of enemies within the county bureaucracy and county staff. I don't know whether that might have spilled over to Capizzi or to Gates in some way that I'm not really aware of, but I know he had a style where he had a tendency to micro-manage and had a tendency to be in battle with Ernie Schneider. It was sort of legendary among county employees not to cross Roger Stanton because he could be very mean spirited. He was also very bright and really sometimes could be pretty hard on staff publicly. I heard many stories about his behavior privately with county employees that left them shaking in their boots. So whether in that context, Roger Stanton was not very well liked by the inner circle, the county department heads, because of that style, I'm not sure.

MADIGAN: You don't have any idea or any specific reason why Capizzi would all of a sudden authorize his people to unleash all of their investigative powers to try to get something on him?

STEINER: I believe that Mike Capizzi's investigators in the aftermath of the bankruptcy probably felt that Roger Stanton was very much involved in the decision making and perhaps had some culpability for the bankruptcy. And I believe that maybe some of that was fed to them by Eileen Walsh and perhaps others that might have had an ax to grind with Roger Stanton. I believe a lot of information given to the District Attorney's Office was very disparaging of Roger Stanton. Maybe that's the reason they decided to go after him because they felt that he was pretty culpable for the bankruptcy. Any of the questions that I got from the Grand Jury, from the SEC and from the DA investigators seemed to always come back to, really, sort of 'Get Stanton.'

MADIGAN: You mentioned Eileen Walsh. What interaction did she have with him?

STEINER: She was head of the Public Finance section of the CAO's office. She was critical of Stanton in a *Los Angeles Times* article where she alluded that there might have been 'play for pay' or Roger putting pressure on her to secure Merrill Lynch's services or to pick a particular underwriter.

MADIGAN: Did you get offered any campaign contributions by Merrill Lynch?

STEINER: I went down to the Pacific Stock Exchange and saw the stock exchange. Merrill Lynch had a lunch there. My campaign received contributions from Merrill Lynch on two different occasions, $500 each time, which is the limit.

MADIGAN: Did you have any meetings, or lunches, or required meetings with Bob Citron?

STEINER: Yes, I had meetings with Bob Citron. He had good reason to be proud of his accomplishments. We had no reason to doubt his abilities, which were sort of legendary around the county before I was with the Board of Supervisors. But he was kind of eccentric, Bob Citron was. As long as he was doing a great job in terms of interest and so forth.

MADIGAN: This happened shortly after you were appointed. Could you tell me, to the best of your recollection what happened?

STEINER: Yes. I was appointed on March 15, 1993. We realized things were going south in November of 1994, about a month before the bankruptcy. All this stuff with John Moorlach was pretty much seen as being politics. Nobody paid much attention and that included the press. So when the bankruptcy hit, it was declared December 6, 1994, then in 1995 all the finger pointing was taking place and of course, I'd been pretty much a new supervisor. In April of 1994, I had some discomfort over what I was reading in the newspapers about John Moorlach's complaints about Bob Citron's investment practices. So I asked Eileen Walsh to do me a favor since I'd known her a long time. I asked her to write a letter to Bob Citron asking him about some of his investment practices, some of the controversy and asking him to answer it. I wasn't even sure of the kind of questions to ask because it's so technical. So Eileen said that she would draft that letter for me, which she did. And in the context of that, several county officials found out about it and came to my office and gave me all these reasons why there was no need to feel uncomfortable about Robert Citron's investment practices. The earnings of interest, the rating agencies giving us the top rating, the amount of cash on deposit in the investment pool. And just that it would be counterproductive to send the letter.

The letter wasn't sent and then six months later it became public, so there was a lot of speculation about why I didn't send that letter.

Well, almost another year went by, in the fall of 1995, probably around November. I'd been to the district attorneys office and I'm not real sure of the sequence, but they had pretty much informed me that it looked like the grand jury was going to issue Willful Misconduct in Office charges against us. Roger Stanton and myself.

I remember sitting with Wally Wade and just being absolutely devastated. That's when it occurred to me. I felt a personal feeling of betrayal because I had worked so closely with the DA's staff as Director of Orangewood, Director of Albert Sitton Home. I worked with John Conley, Bill Evans and Maury Evans on all sorts of child sexual abuse issues and new programs. I had been endorsed by Mike (Capizzi) in my election and he said he was 100% behind me. I'd contributed money to his election. So the last thing in the world that I expected was to be caught up in this. I told Wally Wade how heartbreaking it was for me to think that someone would think that I would willfully try to hurt the county. When obviously, my career in the county had been to try be a very positive influence with Orangewood.

So that's about the time I hired Al Stokke to represent me to see if maybe the Grand Jury action could be stopped. I was using my own funds from the campaign. It so happened that I was up in Sacramento in the Capitol, and I got a phone call. It was from a person within the District Attorney's Office, a longtime friend, who told me that there was still a chance to stop this train that was going down the tracks. I said 'What do you mean' and they said 'Well Bill, there's just a feeling within the district attorney's office that you're not being forthright, that you're covering up for Roger Stanton.' They thought Roger talked me out of sending the letter, which would somehow have prevented what happened. And I said 'What do you mean?' and they said 'Well, you really ought to get over and talk with them and clarify any of your other previous statements to Rusty Hodges or the DA investigators.

MADIGAN: Was Rusty Hodges in charge?

STEINER: Yes, and Mike Major. And so I flew back and I went over to meet with Wally Wade and Rusty Hodges in a room to talk 'man to man' to see whether this thing was going to be stopped. They told me there was no tape recorder going on and I could speak very frankly to them. I said 'Well, I just want to clarify some of my previous comments," which I did.

What this friend of mine told me was that they thought I was covering up for Stanton. Stanton knew about the letter that I did not send to Robert Citron. Something they had talked me out of sending and some way there was a nexus to obstructing and causing a lot of actions to occur which resulted in the bankruptcy, if you stretch it a long ways.

So, I wasn't real close to Roger Stanton, but I had absolutely no reason to burn him and we became quite close during the year and a half that we fought this battle together. He was always very supportive and friendly to me when I was the Director of the Children's home. So there was no way that I was going to protect him just because he was my pal, but at the same time I wasn't going to burn him.

MADIGAN: But did he have anything to do with this?

STEINER: Absolutely not. He never even knew about the letter and I told that to Wally and to Rusty Hodges. And I almost felt like they were disappointed, you know, because for some reason, they seemed to be sort of consumed that Roger was the key, key culpable player in this whole thing.

MADIGAN: How could Roger have been any more or less culpable than Citron or anybody else, in terms of obstruction?

STEINER: I don't know. Other than the fact that I think they felt he was involved with the 'play to pay,' that he had relations to Jeff Leifer, a financial advisor. Eileen Walsh was feeding them a lot of information regarding Roger Stanton's style of doing things. And I guess they felt that maybe Roger was a key person in talking Steiner out of sending that letter. So I told them that absolutely that was not the case and to this day I really feel that the district attorney's office knew that I had another life. I got that appointment in three days by the governor and I wasn't seeking it. I had a very good position previously and I think they really thought that like Gaddi (Vasquez) did, in September or October that I'd resign and it would clear the way to prosecute and go after Roger Stanton.

Wally Wade explained at length that they didn't need a really high standard of proof to prove Willful Misconduct in Office, but he felt quite confident that it was going to happen. He led me to believe that it was the grand jury that was driving the train on Willful Misconduct in Office, but we all know that really wasn't the case.

MADIGAN: The DA drives the grand jury.

STEINER: Yes, and we know that now, but I didn't know it at that time. So I told them all this and so then of course I guess they didn't get what they wanted to hear and of course, a few weeks later, the second of December, the Willful Misconduct in Office charges were leveled against me and I did not resign. I decided to stick it out and I don't think they expected that the board would appropriate all this money to defend us. To this day I feel that the DA's office felt I would resign and get out of the way so they could get Stanton. They knew I had another life and my interest was more in working with abused kids than in politics.

MADIGAN: What did Gaddi Vasquez say to you? Did he decide to resign when he found out or had he already decided that it was a bad idea to stay in as Supervisor.

STEINER: Gaddi told me publicly that the reason he was going to resign was that the things that he wanted to do to get the county positioned, to get out of the bankruptcy and to go to Wall Street to recapitalize, had been achieved. Measure R had not been passed, but the workout proceeded anyway. The settlement agreement had been done with all the pool participants. So Gaddi told me publicly, to my face that he thought that probably this was the time for him to leave. He suggested fairly forcefully that I should resign with him. He suggested I do that. Really, I alluded to the feeling that if I stuck around and got this Willful Misconduct thing hung around my neck, that I would be damaged goods and I would have so much baggage that I could find myself at sixty years of age unable to get a job within the county.

And my self-esteem was just absolutely hammered from going through all this. So I seriously considered resigning. I even asked Wally Wade how soon the Grand Jury would make their Willful Misconduct charge, so I could make my decision whether to resign or not.

But I think Gaddi felt that this thing was coming down the pike and he did not want it hung around his neck. It was hung around Roger's and mine and therefore he decided to get out. All of us really felt Gaddi had been tipped off that the DA was going to do this.

MADIGAN: Do you think it's because he was law enforcement?

STEINER: I think that Gaddi had a strong relationship with Mike Capizzi. I think Gaddi when he was Chairman of the Board was talking with Mike Capizzi. I think Gaddi was very instrumental in this troika being formed and I think there was a lot of back door communication, which I don't know the nature of it all, between Gates, Capizzi and Vasquez.

MADIGAN: So do you think someone came to Gaddi and said, 'Look, it's time for you to dodge this bullet?'

STEINER: Absolutely, and I heard that from many different sources.

MADIGAN: And they came to you and you said, 'Well, let me think about it.'

STEINER: Yes. Well, no, I broached it. Gaddi suggested to me that I ought to go out with him at the same time. But then when I sat down with Wally Wade and realized that they were going to actually do this to me, then I broached the fact that, well, what's the time line in case I would want to resign before the grand jury did this, which would make it moot and they wouldn't do it against me, but then I decided to stick it out and fight it.

MADIGAN: And effectively you won because you did the unexpected and you stopped the train?

STEINER: Yes. To this day I don't understand the dynamics that occurred within the district attorney's office. I would love to talk to somebody who would give me the straight scoop on why I got swept up in this. Because I've had people who have alluded to me, from the district attorney's office, that they felt it was an outrage.

MADIGAN: During the period of time that this was going on, were there any particularly egregious or outrageous acts that the DA did or tried to do, such as surveilling you, or telephone records or anything like that?

STEINER: I don't know. I was told that they would never occur, but you know I got led down the primrose path. I should have known better because I've never been accused of a crime in my whole life and I'm sixty-one years old. And so I went in and sat down with the district attorney investigators with no lawyer and talked and talked and talked and answered all their questions. I tried to be really helpful to them to get to the truth as I saw it. I was a voluntary witness before the grand jury. I shouldn't have gone over there.

Roger didn't go over there, but I did, and I was absolutely stunned at the tone of the questioning before the grand jury. I would have to say Wally Wade treated me professionally, but Jan Nolan was unbelievably condescending. Obviously, there were marching orders for all of these folks.

I don't know where the marching orders came from, but I assume they came from Mike Capizzi. I ran into Maury Evans who's been a friend for years at the Officer's Club at El Toro and I felt like he still believed in me and knew in his heart that I would never do anything. I think John Conley always knew I would never do anything to hurt the county. I think there was some embarrassment within the DA's office over this.

But, I just thought of one thing that could have totally pissed off Mike Capizzi and Brad Gates to go after Roger. I just thought of it and you've probably already been told. Roger did not want to support Measure R and both Brad Gates and Mike Capizzi and Bill Popejoy and all of them were obsessed with the fact that Measure R, the half cent sales tax, had to pass or the county was going to come to a crashing halt. Bill Popejoy said it'd be a third world country. Well, Roger was very anti Measure R and spoke out against it and so forth. And of course Mike Capizzi and Brad Gates sat in my office, one on one side of me and one on the other and put a huge squeeze play on me to 'do the right thing' and support Measure R, although it was political suicide and I'd probably never be re-elected for supporting a tax increase in Orange County. And that was before there were any Willful Misconduct charges, so whether that was a motivating factor for 'getting Stanton' I don't know, but I know they were very concerned that their bureaucracies would not be impacted, the Sheriff's Department and the District Attorney's Office, you know what I mean? By budget cuts.

MADIGAN: Did they come to you to sort of make some trade-offs? What were they trying to say? Did Mike Capizzi ever say; 'Well, you know, you control us but we also control you. You control our budget, we control your freedom?'

STEINER: No, not in so many words. I just don't know. To this day I've always been courteous to Mike Capizzi. Roger Stanton was going for the jugular vein and was highly critical of Capizzi and hated him and it came through in newspaper stories over and over again. I never felt there was a percentage in doing that. So even when I've seen Michael Capizzi at social events, even sitting at a table with he and Sandy, I've always been polite.

MADIGAN: But you're always polite with everybody.

STEINER: Well, you know it was almost like this man was in just complete denial that he had practically destroyed my life. I really thought, well, I felt a couple of times like jumping off the fifth floor of the Hall of Administration. That's how terrible it was. And I almost felt like he was in denial. He never would even act like he had done anything to me at all, you know?

MADIGAN: What has this done to your personal life?

STEINER: Well, I'm OK now. I'm in great shape now. I left the Board on a really good note. I completed my term of office. I'm sixty-two and going back to my work in child abuse and neglect. At the time, it was the most devastating thing that happened in my whole life.

I spent $14,000 for Al Stokke's services before the County indemnified me. I didn't get that back. Then the County spent another $250,000 of the taxpayers money for defending just me.

What did it do to me personally? I think it took some years off my life. Doug DeCinces was my campaign Chairman for several elections. He was concerned about my health. Doug got me into Harbor UCLA Medical Center at the height of this thing. I was up until 2:00 or 3:00 in the morning then at 5:30 or 6:00 in the morning I went out to read the newspaper. Seven days a week.

Doug DeCinces was concerned about my physical health. My emotional health, my mental health, my self-esteem was shattered. I have five children, all of them grew up in Orange County. It was embarrassing to read about yourself in the newspaper and to be caricatured in *The Register*.

MADIGAN: Did anyone serve any search warrants?

STEINER: No.

MADIGAN: Did anyone come into your offices during the night?

STEINER: There was always speculation that the offices were bugged. Always speculation. I don't know if I'm paranoid or not, but it seemed like they always knew what the Board of Supervisors was thinking. I was never able to figure that out.

MADIGAN: Do you think that when the DA's office files charges they expect, more or less, that the people who they're filing against are going to cower and resign?

STEINER: Oh sure.

MADIGAN It didn't happen in this case. Is it possible that this entire thing was a miscalculation that was based upon information that just didn't pan out?

STEINER: Yes.

MADIGAN: Would you characterize it as a misguided effort?

STEINER: It was a total miscalculation. Because I think Mike felt empowered by his reputation as a crusader against corrupt politicians. And I think he felt that not only did he have the public's support, but everybody pretty much folded. With me I think they definitely felt that I would not stay around for this battle.

MADIGAN: Do you think that Mike Capizzi prosecuted the Supervisors for personal gain, for the enhancement of his career?

STEINER: Yes, I believe that's exactly what happened.

MADIGAN: Do you think that's kind of a severe twist of the badge?

STEINER: Yes. I believe it was prosecutorial misconduct. There is awesome power in prosecutor and therefore justice is very precarious because of the tremendous power of the prosecutor. Al Stokke and all of us felt that a lot of evidence was withheld from the grand jury, exculpatory evidence and the grand jury was manipulated into even issuing this Willful Misconduct charge. I mean, they went back to a statute that was something like a hundred years old.

MADIGAN: Do you believe the District Attorney had the authority to accept money from Merrill Lynch to stop the Grand Jury Investigation of their involvement in the bankruptcy? They accepted $30 million.

STEINER: Yes, they did that.

MADIGAN Do you believe he had that right, that power?

STEINER: We were in San Francisco at the Goldman Sachs office, Supervisor Jim Silva, myself and CEO Jan Mittermaier. We were actually stunned when they walked in, the Goldman Sachs people, and had the wire service stories. The story that Mike Capizzi had let Merrill Lynch basically off the hook with this $30 million bone. Because obviously we felt that there was probably some real significant culpability from the criminal standpoint in the activities that took place. And that obviously the county would have a much stronger position if the heat was kept on Merrill Lynch instead of letting them off the hook. But that was his decision that he could make as an independently elected official. No one on the Board of Supervisors knew about it when he did it.

MADIGAN: Do you believe it was within his job description to be able to stop investigating someone for money?

STEINER: I think that probably it was within his authority. Whether that was right or not, that's the question.

MADIGAN: What about Sheriff Gates? Have you talked to him?

STEINER: I went to his retirement party. Most of my questions revolve around Michael Capizzi's thought processes and whether this was even ethical for him to be involved in this.

I'm not sure where Brad fits in, or if Brad fits in, other than the fact that on more than one occasion, I would indicate to Brad, 'How could your pal do this to me?'

MADIGAN: What did he say?

STEINER: He indicated that he had talked to Mike about my getting caught up in this. I heard there was a huge debate in the district attorney's office about whether I should be caught up in this or not. There were a lot of feelings that they shouldn't have done this.

So, Brad sort of verified that to me.

MADIGAN: Do you think he did intercede with his friend Mike?

STEINER: I asked him to, but I don't know if he did or not.

MADIGAN: During the bankruptcy, did Brad ask for special treatment with respect for the funding for his programs?

STEINER: He got special treatment.

MADIGAN: What did he get?

STEINER: He had very few cuts compared to other departments.

MADIGAN: Why was that?

STEINER: Because his department was pretty much bullet proof, due to the force of his personality, his relationships."

END OF EXCERPT

The Defense Strategy

In a recent interview, former Supervisor Steiner's attorney, Allan Stokke, shared his thoughts regarding a possible motivation of the DA's office:

> "I think the District Attorney may have felt that he was going to be dragged into the bankruptcy fiasco. He had supported each of the members of the Board of Supervisors and their political campaigns and when a bankruptcy takes place there's just a natural feeling on the part of the citizens to say 'Let's just get rid of everybody that was involved. However, if the District Attorney could separate himself from all the politicians, then his lack of action prior to the bankruptcy doesn't look so negative."

The Aftermath

According to the *LA Times*, Citron's investments resulted in a loss of $1.64 billion to the almost 200 schools, cities, water and sewer districts who invested in the pool. In 1998, Merrill Lynch agreed to pay the county $437.1 million to settle a lawsuit that accused them of giving Citron bad advice.

Approximately $860.7 million was recovered.

* * *

The Bankruptcy

5

The Candidates

In July 1995, corporate lawyer Scott Baugh was introduced to Republican Congressman Dana Rohrabacher. Before the end of that year he'd been elected to the Assembly and became the target of a grand jury investigation lasting more than four years.

Orange County prosecutor Michael Capizzi had spent his entire career relentlessly pursuingt politicians. According to his resume, he obtained the indictment and conviction of 40 county political figures during his 33 years as a prosecutor. A Republican, he seemed to go after a lot of Democrats, so it was definitely an advantage to be a Republican in Orange County.

In 1995, Capizzi disclosed his intention to run for Attorney General. By all appearances, he planned to win the election using the same system which had served him so well in the past: indict, hold press conferences, negotiate plea bargains, declare victory, then move to Sacramento.

But what happens when there's no case to prosecute? That question is best answered by key documents and the parties involved. This chapter contains the original indictment, an interview with Assemblyman Baugh, an interview with defense attorney Allan H. Stokke and the summaries and opinions of Superior Court Judges James Smith and Francisco Briseno:

IN THE SUPERIOR COURT OF THE STATE OF CALIFORNIA

IN AND FOR THE COUNTY OF ORANGE

THE PEOPLE OF THE STATE OF CALIFORNIA, Plaintiff, vs. SCOTT R. BAUGH, Defendant(s)	)	CASE NO. 96ZF0020 **INDICTMENT**

THE GRAND JURY OF THE COUNTY OF ORANGE, STATE OF CALIFORNIA, BY THIS INDICTMENT, hereby accuses the aforenamed defendant(s) of violating the law at and within the County of Orange as follows:

COUNT 1: On or about and between September 21 and October 19, 1995, SCOTT R. BAUGH, in violation of Section 127 of the Penal Code (SUBORNATION OF PERJURY), a FELONY, did willfully and unlawfully procure another person, to wit, DANIEL TRAXLER, to commit perjury in that he procured said person, who was to declare and certify under penalty of perjury in a case in which such declaration, and certification is permitted by law under penalty of perjury, to wit, an Officeholder, Candidate and Controlled Committee Campaign Statement - Long Form, dated October 19, 1995 and filed with the Orange County Registrar of Voters October 19, 1995, to willfully state as true a material matter which said person knew to be false, to wit: that Scott Baugh made a $1,000 campaign contribution on September 21 and returned it to himself the same day, while concealing that Richard and Laurie Campbell made a contribution of $1,000 on or about September 15, 1995, and that their $1,000 contribution was returned on September 21, 1995.

COUNT 2: On or about October 19, 1995, SCOTT R. BAUGH, in violation of Section 84211(f) of the Government Code, a MISDEMEANOR, did willfully and unlawfully, as a person required to file a Candidate Campaign Statement, fail to disclose required information concerning a $1,000 campaign contribution made by Richard and Laurie Campbell on September 14, 1995, in a Candidate Campaign Statement filed pursuant to Government Code Section 84200.8.

COUNT 3: On or about October 19, 1995, SCOTT R. BAUGH, in violation of Section 84211(j) of the Government Code, a MISDEMEANOR, did willfully and unlawfully, as a person required to file a Candidate Campaign Statement, fail to disclose required information concerning a $1,000 expenditure made to return a campaign contribution to Richard and Laurie Campbell on September 21, 1995, in a Candidate Campaign Statement filed pursuant to Government Code Section 84200.8.

COUNT 4: On or about October 19, 1995, SCOTT R. BAUGH, in violation of Section 84211(j) of the Government Code, a MISDEMEANOR, did willfully and unlawfully, as a person required to file a Candidate Campaign Statement, fail to disclose required information concerning the return, on or about October 3, 1995 to Longfin Tackle, and to Longfin Charter, of two $10,000 campaign loans previously made on or about September 28, 1995 by The Longfin, in a Candidate Campaign Statement filed pursuant to Government Code Section 84200.8.

COUNT 5: On or about October 19, 1995, SCOTT R. BAUGH, in violation of Section 84211(j) of the Government Code, a MISDEMEANOR, did willfully and unlawfully, as a person required to file a Candidate Campaign Statement, fail to disclose required information concerning the return, on or about October 2, 1995 to Donna Mailler, of a $7,000 campaign loan previously made on or about September 28, 1995 by Donna and John Mailler, in a Candidate Campaign Statement filed pursuant to Government Code Section 84200.8.

COUNT 6: On or about August 25, 1995, SCOTT R. BAUGH, in violation of Section 84300(a) of the Government Code, a MISDEMEANOR, did willfully and unlawfully, as a person defined as a Candidate in Government Code Section 82007, receive a campaign contribution of one hundred dollars or more in cash, to wit: a $8,800 cash campaign contribution from Adel Zeidan on or about August 25, 1995, and reported this contribution as received on September 15, 1995 in a Candidate Campaign Statement filed on October 19, 1995, pursuant to Government Code Section 84200.8.

COUNT 7: On or about and between November 1 and November 6, 1995, SCOTT R. BAUGH, in violation of Section 118 of the Penal Code (PERJURY BY DECLARATION), a FELONY, being a person who, declared and certified under penalty of perjury in a case in which such declaration, and certification is permitted by law under penalty of perjury, to wit, on an Officeholder, Candidate and Controlled Committee Campaign Statement - Long Form, dated November 1, 1995 and filed with the Orange County Registrar of Voters November 6, 1995, did willfully state as true a material matter which he either knew to be false, or which he did not know to be true to wit: (A) that Scott Baugh made a $1,000 campaign contribution on September 21, and returned $1,000 to himself the same day, while concealing that Richard and Laurie Campbell made a contribution of $1,000 on or about September 15, 1995, and that their $1,000 contribution was returned on September 21, 1995; and (B) that two loans from The Longfin and another from Donna and John Mailler, received on or about September 29, 1995, totaling $27,000, were still due and outstanding, when he had repaid them almost immediately.

2

COUNT 8: On or about and between November 1 and November 6, 1995, SCOTT R. BAUGH, in violation of Section 84211(f) of the Government Code, a MISDEMEANOR, did willfully and unlawfully, as a person required to file a Candidate Campaign Statement, fail to disclose required information concerning a $1,000 campaign contribution made by Richard and Laurie Campbell on September 14, 1995, in a Candidate Campaign Statement filed pursuant to Government Code Section 84200.8.

COUNT 9: On or about and between November 1 and November 6, 1995, SCOTT R. BAUGH, in violation of Section 84211(j) of the Government Code, a MISDEMEANOR, did willfully and unlawfully, as a person required to file a Candidate Campaign Statement, fail to disclose required information concerning a $1,000 expenditure made to return a campaign contribution to Richard and Laurie Campbell on September 21, 1995, in a Candidate Campaign Statement filed pursuant to Government Code Section 84200.8.

COUNT 10: On or about and between November 1 and November 6, 1995, SCOTT R. BAUGH, in violation of Section 84211(j) of the Government Code, a MISDEMEANOR, did willfully and unlawfully, as a person required to file a Candidate Campaign Statement, fail to disclose required information concerning the return, on or about October 3, 1995 to Longfin Tackle, and Longfin Charter, of two $10,000 campaign loans previously made on or about September 28, 1995 by The Longfin, in a Candidate Campaign Statement filed pursuant to Government Code Section 84200.8.

COUNT 11: On or about and between November 1 and November 6, 1995, SCOTT R. BAUGH, in violation of Section 84211(j) of the Government Code, a MISDEMEANOR, did willfully and unlawfully, as a person required to file a Candidate Campaign Statement, fail to disclose required information concerning the return, on or about October 2, 1995 to Donna Mailler, of a $7,000 campaign loan previously made on or about September 28, 1995 by Donna and John Mailler, in a Candidate Campaign Statement filed pursuant to Government Code Section 84200.8.

COUNT 12: On or about November 28, 1995, SCOTT R. BAUGH, in violation of Section 118 of the Penal Code (PERJURY BY DECLARATION), a FELONY, being a person who, declared and certified under penalty of perjury in a case in which such declaration, and certification is permitted by law under penalty of perjury, to wit, on an Amendment to Campaign Disclosure Statement attached to an Officeholder, Candidate and Controlled Committee Campaign Statement - Long Form, dated November 28, 1995 and filed with the Orange County Registrar of Voters November 28, 1995, did willfully state as true a material matter which he either knew to be false, or which he did not know to be true to wit: stating that the reason for the Second Amendment to his campaign statement dated November 28, was "One contributor of $1000 was inadvertently omitted."

/ / /

3

COUNT 13: On or about November 28, 1995, SCOTT R. BAUGH, in violation of Section 84300(b) of the Government Code, a MISDEMEANOR, did willfully and unlawfully, as a person defined as a Candidate in Government Code Section 82007, make an expenditure of one hundred dollars or more in cash, to wit: a $1,000 cash return of campaign contribution to Richard and Laurie Campbell on September 21, 1995, and reported this return of contribution as made on September 21, 1995 in a Candidate Campaign Statement filed on November 28, 1995, pursuant to Government Code Section 84200.8.

COUNT 14: On or about and between November 16 and November 17, 1995, SCOTT R. BAUGH, in violation of Section 84211(f) of the Government Code, and within the meaning of Government Code Section 84216(b), a MISDEMEANOR, did willfully and unlawfully, as a person required to file a Candidate Campaign Statement, fail to disclose required information concerning a $2,000 loan used for political purposes, made by Ahmad Zaidan on or about November 9, 1995, in a Candidate Campaign Statement filed pursuant to Government Code Section 84200.8.

COUNT 15: On or about and between November 16 and November 17, 1995, SCOTT R. BAUGH, in violation of Section 84211(f) of the Government Code, and within the meaning of Government Code Section 84216(b), a MISDEMEANOR, did willfully and unlawfully, as a person required to file a Candidate Campaign Statement, fail to disclose required information concerning a $3,000 loan used for political purposes, made by Donna Loren and Dennis Harnisch on or about November 10, 1995, in a Candidate Campaign Statement filed pursuant to Government Code Section 84200.8.

COUNT 16: On or about and between January 9 and January 10, 1996, SCOTT R. BAUGH, in violation of Section 84211(f) of the Government Code, and within the meaning of Government Code Section 84216(b), a MISDEMEANOR, did willfully and unlawfully, as a person required to file a Candidate Campaign Statement, fail to disclose all required information concerning a $6,000 loan used for political purposes, reportedly made by Scott Baugh on November 12, 1995, but actually supported in large part by a $3,000 loan made by Donna Loren and Dennis Harnisch on November 10, 1995 and another $2,000 loan made by Ahmad Zaidan on November 9, 1995, in a Candidate Campaign Statement filed pursuant to Government Code Section 84200.8.

COUNT 17: On or about and between January 9 and January 10, 1996, SCOTT R. BAUGH, in violation of Section 84211(j) of the Government Code, a MISDEMEANOR, did willfully and unlawfully, as a person required to file a Candidate Campaign Statement, fail to disclose required information concerning the return, on or about and between November 16, 1995 and November 21, 1995 to Ahmad Zaidan, of a $2,000 campaign loan previously made on or about November 9, 1995 by Ahmad Zaidan, in a Candidate Campaign Statement filed pursuant to Government Code Section 84200.8.

COUNT 18: On or about and between September 20 and September 21, 1995, SCOTT R. BAUGH, in violation of Section 87201 of the Government Code, a MISDEMEANOR, did willfully and unlawfully, as a candidate for elected state office, required to file a Statement of Economic Interests, pursuant to Government Code Section 87201, fail to disclose a $6,000 loan from Wendy Ward/Longfin Travel Adventures, made September 1, 1995, in a Statement of Economic Interests.

COUNT 19: On or about and between January 13, 1996 and January 17, 1996, SCOTT R. BAUGH, in violation of Section 118 of the Penal Code (PERJURY BY DECLARATION), a FELONY, being a person who, declared and certified under penalty of perjury in a case in which such declaration, and certification is permitted by law under penalty of perjury, to wit, on a Form 721 Statement of Economic Interests, dated January 13, 1996 and filed with the Orange County Registrar of Voters January 17, 1996, as required by Government Code section 87202, did willfully state as true a material matter which he either knew to be false, or which he did not know to be true to wit: (A) the omission of a $6,000 loan from Wendy Ward/Longfin Travel Adventures; (B) the omission of a $2,000 loan from Ahmad Zaidan;and (c) the omission of a $3,000 loan from Donna Loren and Dennis Harnisch, all on a Form 721, Statement of Economic Interests.

COUNT 20: On or about and between January 13 and January 17, 1996, SCOTT R. BAUGH, in violation of Section 87202 of the Government Code, a MISDEMEANOR, did willfully and unlawfully, as a person who had been elected to state office, required to file a Statement of Economic Interests, pursuant to Government Code Section 87202, fail to disclose a $6,000 loan from Wendy Ward/Longfin Travel Adventures, made September 1, 1995, in a Statement of Economic Interests.

COUNT 21: On or about and between January 13 and January 17, 1996, SCOTT R. BAUGH, in violation of Section 87202 of the Government Code, a MISDEMEANOR, did willfully and unlawfully, as a person who had been elected to state office, required to file a Statement of Economic Interests, pursuant to Government Code Section 87202, fail to disclose a $2,000 loan from Ahmad Zaidan, made on or about November 9, 1995, in a Statement of Economic Interests.

/ / /

/ / /

/ / /

/ / /

/ / /

/ / /

COUNT 22: On or about and between January 13 and January 17, 1996, SCOTT R. BAUGH, in violation of Section 87202 of the Government Code, a MISDEMEANOR, did willfully and unlawfully, as a person who had been elected to state office, required to file a Statement of Economic Interests, pursuant to Government Code Section 87202, fail to disclose a $3,000 loan from Donna Loren and Dennis Harnisch, made November 10, 1995, in a Statement of Economic Interests.

Pursaunt to Penal Code Section 1054.5(b), the People are hereby informally requesting that defense counsel provide discovery to the People as required by Penal Code Section 1054.3.

DATED: March 21, 1996

A TRUE BILL

DONALD WECKER, Foreman, Grand Jury
County of Orange, State of California
for the year 1996-1997

BY: ______________________
GUY N. ORMES
DEPUTY DISTRICT ATTORNEY
96F00220

BY: ______________________
JOHN ANDERSON
DEPUTY DISTRICT ATTORNEY

- - - WITNESSES EXAMINED BEFORE THE GRAND JURY - - -

Laurie Campbell
Kendrick Campbell
Jeffrey Butler
James Righeimer
Jeff Nielson
Wendy Ward
Daniel Traxler
Adel Zeidan
Danielle Madison
Catherine Rayner
Linda Moulton-Patterson
Lysa Pisarski
Douglas Miller
Randy Sorley
George Rundall

Justin Wallin
Mohammad Zeidan
Ahmad Zeidan
Eric Zehnder
Donna Loren
Dennis Harnisch
Tina Vega
Bernadette Bellah
Susan Blanco
Daniel Powers
James Tamura
Darla Davis
Robert Harper
Mark Denny
Jeffrey Gibson
Richard Martin

Presented by the Foreman of the Grand Jury of the County of Orange, State of California, for the year 1996-1997, in the presence of the Grand Jury, to the Superior Court of the State of California, in and for the County of Orange, and filed as a record of this court this 21st day of March, 1996.

ALAN SLATER, EXECUTIVE OFFICER
and Clerk of the Superior Court
of the State of California, in and
for the County of Orange

BY: [signature]
DEPUTY ~~COUNTY~~ COURT CLERK

MICHAEL R. CAPIZZI, DISTRICT ATTORNEY
of the County of Orange, State of California

BY: [signature]
GUY N. ORMES
Deputy District Attorney

7

Interview with Assemblyman Scott Baugh

On July 28, 1999, I interviewed Assemblyman Baugh at his Huntington Beach District Office. During an at times emotional hour, he talked about his ordeal:

MM: What was it that opened your eyes to the possibility of being a public servant?

SB: This may surprise you. I was dating my wife, Wendy, in 1995 and I told her I was interested in politics, mostly from a national perspective. She had met some fellow that came into the store where she worked who said he worked on Congressman Rohrabacher's campaign. This gentleman told her to tell me that if I was interested in becoming involved in politics I should come to downtown Huntington Beach that weekend, it was in July of '95, to meet Congressman Rohrabacher.

MM: And you were an attorney at that time?

SB: Yes, I was in-house counsel for Union Pacific Railroad.

MM: So basically you were living in the corporate world?

SB: Right. And I had no political involvement to speak of. And I went down that weekend in July and met Congressman Rohrabacher and they started the recall of Doris Allen. I really didn't know who Doris Allen was. I was not involved in local politics or state politics. I knew that Doris Allen had cut a deal with Willie Brown, I was aware of that, but I didn't particularly understand the dynamics of state politics. I was unaware in large part that she represented Huntington Beach. I knew she was from Cypress and I probably voted for her, though I have no memory of it. In any event, I started gathering signatures as part of that recall and I thought that was pretty interesting. I was pretty engaged in that. I know a lot of merchants in downtown Huntington Beach and I walked up and down the sidewalks and got people to sign the petition for recall.

MM: That was in the summer of '95?

SB: Yes. July of '95. Then I left on vacation for about three weeks and I came back and the recall was still going. I got a phone call the first week of August from a woman named Hope Durio, who was a volunteer on Congressman Rohrabacher's campaign. She asked me if I wanted to run for office and I said 'What office?' and she said 'To replace Doris Allen.' and I said 'Isn't Jim Righeimer running for that seat?' She told me that Jim was dropping out of the race because he was getting married and he just couldn't put the whole campaign together at that time. And I said 'Why would they support me for this office?' and she said they were looking for someone who was articulate, conservative and could raise $100,000 I said 'I'm interested. What do I do?'

I proceeded to have conversations with Congressman Rohrabacher's campaign manager, Rhonda Carmony, and Jim Righeimer. They interviewed me and basically were seeing if I was really a conservative. I told them my views and apparently I passed their test.

The following week they arranged for me to meet with Congressman Rohrabacher. I was extremely excited to meet the Congressman and have a conversation with him because I'd only met him briefly. So we had lunch together and we talked about my philosophy. He grilled me in depth. It was a wonderful conversation about what I believed in and I had no idea whether it fit his definition of what a conservative was. We had a very nice conversation and he asked me about my ability to raise the money and he advised me that a lot of people promise they can deliver money and a lot of times they don't come through. First of all he told me he liked my philosophy and if I could raise $100,000 I would be considered for his endorsement. So I went to work, calling all my friends. I went to my home town where I grew up.

MM: Where was that?

SB: In Redding, where I was very involved in a church and my mother and some friends from church put on a big party and we raised somewhere between $25,000 and $30,000. I came back to Huntington Beach and was asking all my friends to help out. It was an exciting time. I was an attorney for Union Pacific Railroad, so I went through Union Pacific and I asked those folks for help. There's a little market near my house down by the beach. I was very good friends with the owner and I asked him for a contribution.

Just by way of history, I had done a lot of legal work for free for people in the neighborhood and he was very appreciative of that. He wanted to give me a large contribution and that was one of the ones I got in trouble over. He gave me $8,800. in cash. I had no idea you couldn't take cash. In fact I really didn't know what the rules were. I was told to go out and raise $100,000 and that's what I was doing.

MM: But you put the money in a campaign account?

SB: Yes. A campaign account was opened for me by Congressman Rohrabacher's staff. Adel Zeidan gave me the contribution and I drove it immediately to the bank because I didn't want to hang on to the cash. I deposited it directly into the campaign account. I reported every penny of it.

I ended up having to pay a $16,000 fine for that and I was charged with crimes on more than one occasion for that transaction. What was always odd to me on that one is that the purpose of the prohibition against accepting cash is twofold. People don't report cash and secondly people launder cash. All of this money was fully reported and none of it was laundered, so the entire spirit of the law was complied with and yet the DA just tried to demonize that act. It was simply a mistake. We didn't know you couldn't take cash.

In any event, I continued raising the $100,000. Another crime I was charged with, my girlfriend, now my wife Wendy, loaned me $6,000. We banked at the same bank and she deposited the check into my account. I never even handled the check. I got charged with a misdemeanor and two felonies for that transaction.

MM: Based on what?

SB: Well, I subsequently learned that a candidate is not supposed to accept any loans into their personal account. Again, I was unaware of that prohibition. I reported that loan as a personal loan on my economic interest statement as required by law. The DA charged me with perjury for calling it a personal loan when it was really a political loan. I also got charged with a felony for not disclosing it on my campaign reports as a political loan. To me, that's just like the death penalty for a traffic violation. I disclosed the loan. I didn't do it the right way and I got two felonies and a misdemeanor for that. A lot of that happened.

MM: Let me ask you something. Your introduction to politics appears to have been very positive. While all of these things were going on, before there were any charges, before any of these other problems started, was it just one positive thing after another happening which caused you to win the election? Did anything negative happen along the way?

SB: Well, I'm going to explain this to you. I'll leave the tape on but I'll put the caveat that this is off the record for now. Just to give you a complete understanding.

When the Republicans put a Democrat on the ballot, I took great exception to that. I couldn't believe that you could do that. I didn't understand why you would even want to do that. I know now that it's pretty clear why they wanted to do that. I just thought it was wrong. It was deceptive and the day that it happened, I wanted to withdraw from the whole race. I ran because I wanted to do good. I wanted to serve the community and do what was right and to me that wasn't right.

But all the experts say 'Well that's how things are done.' I remember my campaign manager, Todd Nugent came over to my house and we walked down by the beach. I said 'I don't want to run under these circumstances.' He said 'You know that's really not your doing. You put your hand to the plow here and you need to continue on.'

You ask was it one positive thing after another, well right off the bat, I did not think that was appropriate. Putting that aside, it was all positive. The reaction I got from all my friends and colleagues and their contributions and reading up on literature and issues. It's amazing what you don't know on issues and how to address issues and deal with the press. I was green as could be.

MM: Wasn't that your own party?

SB: Yes, trying to make sure that I would win. I just thought it was unfortunate. And you see, the Democrat was thrown off the ballot and I still won by a large margin. The whole effort was not even needed. There's nothing illegal with putting a democrat on the ballot. I just didn't like it. I thought it was underhanded.

So, the whole experience of running was very positive. I remember we went down to the Central Committee when we had to give our first candidate's debate. I didn't know very many people down there other than the people who were helping me. Right before I went down to give my speech, Jim Righeimer, the fellow who dropped out of the race, was helping me. He said 'What're you going to say?' and I started describing things to him and he said 'Well, if you put a little emphasis here and tell a personal story about this and that, this'll go a lot better.' So I took some personal notes and went in and gave my speech. I don't think I'd ever given a speech of that nature ever. To my shock, people were happy and clapping and yelling. I guess I was hitting the right buttons.

MM: What happened in the election?

SB: The district chose to recall Doris Allen and I was the top vote getter. It was a winner take all for the top vote getter, so I won the election. You've got to bear in mind, in July I met the Congressman, in August I became the candidate and in November I got elected. In that short period of time my whole life changed. I resigned from Union Pacific and got sworn in. Then the investigation started.

MM: When did you first learn of the investigation?

SB: Actually before the election, which was on November 28. On November 18, a Saturday morning, two investigators from the DA's Office came to my house. They were beating on my door.

MM: What time was it?

SB: 7:00 a.m. Around that time. My mother was visiting. She was terrified and wouldn't even go to the door. They were beating on the door. I was getting up to prepare for another speech and a debate. As I came downstairs they continued beating on the door. I opened the door and it was Randy Sorley and Doug Miller from the DA's Office. I asked if I could help them and they said they wanted to ask me a few questions. I said 'Well, you know I've got to take a shower and get ready for a debate. Could you set up an interview or a time and I'll be glad to talk to you.' They said 'No,' they didn't want to do that, they wanted to talk to me right then.

I said, 'You know I can't stop my whole schedule for you fellows. I'm willing to tell you whatever you want to know but I can't do it right now.' They insisted, so I said 'I'll tell you what I'm going to do. I'm going to go up and take a shower and get ready to do what I've got to do. If there's still time, I'll see at that point whether I can talk. So I went up and took a shower, got dressed and came back down and they were still there waiting out front. I had about 15 minutes before I had to leave.

So I said 'I'll be glad to answer your questions,' but before I started I said 'I'm going to give you 15 minutes, if you can't ask me what you need to ask me in 15 minutes, you're going to have to set up an appointment. I looked at one of the investigator's watches and noted what the time was and I said '15 minutes from now you're going to be done.' So they started asking me these questions and I said 'You know I have concerns that you're leaking all this to the *LA Times*. I don't mind telling you what I know, but I need your assurance that there aren't games being played here and you're not just going to turn around and leak this to the *LA Times*.' That interview was recorded and that became an issue later in court. The investigators denied that they were leaking it to the *LA Times*, but we knew better because we had confirmation.

MM: How was it recorded?

SB: They had a tape recorder there.

MM: They showed you the tape recorder?

SB: Yes. They started asking me questions and it got to a point where 15 minutes was up and I said 'I'm leaving,' and they said 'Oh, just another question,' and I said 'No, I'm a lawyer. I know how one more question goes. I'm leaving. They were very upset that I cut them off.

MM: What was the focus of their questions?

SB: They wanted to know if I knew Laurie Campbell. I said "Yes" and they asked 'How long have you known her?'

And I said 'seven or eight years, something like that.' And they were asking about my campaign, how it got started and I told them the same story I was telling you about Jim Righeimer dropping out and trying to raise money. They wanted to know who was putting my campaign together and who orchestrated everything. That was the nature of their questions.

MM: What was your next contact with the DA's Office?

SB: I can't tell you my memory is perfect here, but Randy Sorley called my house again one Sunday night when my parents were in town. I was having dinner with them. He had called a couple of times, once at about 10:30 p.m. and left messages and I became a little irritated with him. I said 'I don't understand what your urgency is. Unless you can describe it to me, I'm going to ask you once again to set up an appointment with me. I'm willing to talk with you, but I don't want you bugging me and my family at home.' There's a transcript of that somewhere.

MM: It was tape recorded?

SB: I didn't know it at the time, but it was being taped. He started arguing with me and I said 'You know, you guys come in here and you beat the crap out of my front door and you scare my mother and then you want me to cooperate with you. I think if you use a little courtesy and set up a meeting, you'll get whatever it is you want.' I didn't talk to him any more that night. I don't remember how we hung up, but they never did call back for an interview. They just kept trying to catch me in awkward positions or moments. I imagine it's their M.O. on how they interview people. I tried to call (DDA) Guy Ormes one time just before the election to try to set something up.

MM: Who initiated that contact? Did Guy Ormes or his office call you?

SB: I don't recall. I know they leaked some story that I was refusing to cooperate. Before the election. That story ran on

Thanksgiving weekend, before the election. I told him I'd be glad to cooperate. I had campaign duties I had to do, but right after the election I'd be glad to talk with him. After the election we knew the grand jury was being started because some of my friends were being subpoenaed.

MM: There was an incident that happened just before Christmas.

SB: Traumatic.

MM: Tell me about that.

SB: Actually it's difficult. On December 22, 1995, I was already elected. I was in the shower getting ready to go meet Assemblyman Bill Morrow. I had a breakfast appointment with him and I once again heard this beating on the front door, which should've been familiar to me. The phone was ringing also. I answered the phone and I think Doug Miller identified himself and said that they had a search warrant and I was supposed to open the door immediately or they would force their way in or something like that. I said 'I'm not dressed. Let me get some clothes on,' and they said 'No, you've got to do it right now.' I didn't see the urgency of it, but I grabbed a robe and went downstairs and opened the door. It was amazing to me. Seven armed guys coming through the front door.

MM: Were their weapons drawn?

SB: No, they asked me if I had any weapons in the house and I said 'No' and one of them pulled his jacket back and showed me his gun and said 'Well there are now.' I thought to myself 'You're a little man inside if you've got to do this.' Maybe that's standard M.O. I didn't know, I just thought it was rather childish and immature. They had a video camera. One guy came in and it was just like the cop show 'Bad boys, bad boys'. It was shocking to me. They handed me the search warrant and I asked for their cards. I wanted to know who they were and I only recognized Miller and Sorley. The rest of them wouldn't give cards, which caused me some concern. I asked one fellow what his name was. He responded by saying 'Helen' in a sarcastic tone. They proceeded to search the house and garage. I went upstairs to get dressed.

It surprised me, maybe this is for their own protection, but they wouldn't let me get dressed alone. It was somewhat invasive to me. I said 'Here's the clothes I'm going to put on. I'm going to go in the bathroom and get dressed.' They said 'No, we're going to have to be here with you.'

So I got dressed there in front of them and then called Bill Morrow and told him I wasn't going to make it. Then I called Al Stokke, my lawyer, and told him what was happening. I didn't know what my rights were. I didn't even know if I could call my lawyer. Al said 'Just cooperate with them.'

The search started at about 7:00 a.m. and went on for about three hours.

MM: Do you remember what the search warrant said?

SB: The search warrant said items related to the campaign, items tending to prove I lived there. Maybe it was standard, maybe it wasn't. I don't know.

I remember they wanted to go into my office upstairs and close the door and I said 'I don't want you to close the door.' I was cooperative. They were asking me questions and I was answering them. They'd find a document and ask me about it and I'd tell them what it was. I had nothing to hide from them, but I wouldn't let them go in and close the door or go in my office alone. I've heard too many stories about things being planted. I just didn't trust the situation, so I stood there. I wasn't in the way or anything. I was just standing in the hallway while they were in my office going through all my documents, including my tax returns. They took tax returns and utility bills and things like that.

When they had gone through the entire home, every nook and cranny, drawers, closets, cupboards, the garage, cabinets, they began to box everything up. Something inside of me that said 'Get a picture of what they're doing.'I didn't know where my camera was, but I had a little plastic camera in my car in the garage, so I went out to the garage and got the camera. I went back in the home and I started taking pictures.

The DA investigators were covering their faces. They didn't want to be photographed and I said 'You know if you guys won't give me identification who you are I'm going to take a picture of who is ransacking my home three days before Christmas. So I took some pictures there and then I went out in front and started taking pictures of all the boxes they were taking out. Two of the investigators came up to me and said they didn't want pictures taken and said they were going to take the camera. I told them the camera was not in their search warrant and I wasn't going to voluntarily give it to them. They said 'Well, you're taking pictures of the evidence,' and I said 'You have the evidence. That should be sufficient.' Two of them came after me and grabbed me and tried to get the camera from me. I can't even tell you what was going through my mind. In situations like that, you just react.

We were being violated. They were trying to grab something

and I didn't know why they wanted it. It's a camera. I'd taken pictures of them. They grabbed me and threw me up against the wall out in front of my house and they were trying to get the camera from me.

Instinctively, I just hunkered down and I wouldn't let them have it. They threw me up against the wall. I had stucco and gouge marks all over my back from this incident. One of them had his arm around my neck and was choking me and I was yelling for my roommate, Ken Eastburn, to call the cops. Obviously they were the cops, but it was just a reaction. We came busting through the front door and as soon as they saw my roommate, they let go and left. They were done. The search was over. I was just taking pictures of the last boxes they were taking out.

Still shocked by the incident, I called the Huntington Beach Police to report what had just happened. My fiancee drove up as they were leaving and she came up to me, but I was having a hard time getting the words out. I was trying to tell her what had happened. They came here and they threw me around. I was so flabbergasted that they could do that for no apparent reason other than they didn't like being photographed doing what they were doing. I walked in the house and I could hardly stand up. They tweaked my back pretty good. Al Stokke came over and I had some friends come over and ... I don't know how to describe it.

I'd heard stories about police brutality. I wasn't beaten up. I was choked a little bit and I had gouge marks on my back. But it occurred to me that these claims of police brutality perhaps were true.

Whereas before I always kind of thought 'Well that's one

version against another,' I was really shocked and shook up by the whole incident. After I disclosed all the photographs to the press and told them what had happened, the DA denied they ever even touched me. They just denied it, collectively denied there was ever an incident. Fortunately for me there was a fellow across the street who witnessed the whole thing. My roommate, who saw them choking me, related his story to the press.

It just shocked me how they could not only come in and violate you, but they could cover it up and deny it ever happened. That incident, more so than being indicted, profoundly affected my view of law enforcement.

That's the incident that occurred December 22, 1995.

MM: Did the Huntington Beach Police Department become involved?

SB: They came down and took a report. They saw where the struggle occurred. They saw the stucco on the ground from the altercation up against the house. They wrote a report up of basically what I told them, but other than that they didn't get involved. I think they referred it over to the AG's Office or the DA's Office and nothing ever came of that report. There were so many things going on, you can only fight so many fires at one time, but nothing ever happened with that.

MM: Did they ever serve any more search warrants at your house?

SB: No. They did another search warrant affidavit for telephone records, but I don't think they ever came to my house again. However, I had friends who watched my house when I was gone and one of them had reported a suspicious vehicle in front of my home. They got the license plate and we learned that it was one of the investigators from the DA's office. What they were doing I don't know.

MM: About when was that?

SB: It was sometime in '96.

MM: That was after you were in office?

SB: Oh yeah, it was way after the search warrant. I think it was even after I was indicted.

The '95 grand jury didn't return an indictment. I don't know why. That was the Merrill Lynch grand jury. The one that indicted Supervisor Bill Steiner. In January '96 I didn't know what was going to happen. My treasurer was calling me and unbeknownst to me was taping my telephone calls.

MM: Tell me about your treasurer, Dan Traxler.

SB: Dan Traxler was a man who Dana Rohrabacher had used as a treasurer and told me to use him. I had one conversation with him and I asked him why he was doing campaign reporting. He said that his tax business was dropping and he wanted to get more involved in political campaign reporting. He said he'd been doing this for Congressman Rohrabacher and I assumed he knew what he was doing.

MM: Was he a tax preparer by profession?

SB: I was told he was a CPA. I learned later that he was a tax preparer and he was not a CPA at all. I really had very little contact with him. I turned all my books over to him. He had asked me about the $8,800. He didn't have a check for that and I told him that it was cash. He told me 'You can't take cash.' I asked him since I already did, what do I do about it? He said 'Well, we'll have to call the FPPC,' and I said 'Go ahead, find out how to fix it.' There was no intent to hide it or anything.

Anyway, he just seemed like a man who was in way over his head. He didn't know the campaign reporting laws and he prepared the reports. The first report was due and he never reviewed it with me. He forged my name to the report and turned it in. That was the report that had all the errors on it.

MM: And you never saw it?

SB: No. I never saw a copy of it and I never saw the final draft. In fact, I had to go down to the Registrar's office after the election to get a copy of it. He never provided it to me.

By that time our relationship was a little strained because of the DA's involvement, but in January of 1996 he called me. Dan Traxler initiated this phone call and it was during this conversation that he brought up the thousand dollars from the husband of the Democratic candidate and I said 'Dan, I don't know what the problem is. You told me that contribution could just be returned and it didn't have to be reported.' He said 'I know. I remember that's what I told you.'

I said 'Dan, you know I never even saw that report.' He said 'I know.' I said 'You know I never signed the report' and he said 'Yeah, I know.' And then he volunteered 'And you ordered me to fix it once you found out the mistakes were there.' so I said 'I don't know what the DA is doing. I don't know what the problem is.'

MM: And that was taped?

SB: That was taped and unbeknownst to me, the DA was sitting there right next to him giving him questions. We learned that later because there's another tape that described it. They were giving him these questions.

There were about eleven transcripts of interviews with Dan Traxler plus my telephone calls that had all this exonerating evidence on it - that I never saw or signed the reports and he gave me wrong advice about the reporting requirements. All of that evidence was hidden from the grand jury. He went into the grand jury and actually said quite the opposite. He said I orchestrated everything and I ordered him to report things a certain way. Later we learned the DA had threatened to charge him with felonies unless he said those things.

I told my lawyer, Al Stokke, what had really happened. I remember going to him and I said 'Al, here's what happened. I can tell you everything I know.' And he said 'Well, that's interesting and I believe you, but it's your word against his. You're a lawyer, you're a politician. The jury will resolve all doubts against you.' I said 'But Al, I didn't do this,' and he said 'I believe you. I'm just telling you what a jury is likely to find.'

After I got indicted, the DA had to turn over all these transcripts. I remember all the boxes came in here to my office and I went over to Kinko's to photocopy so I had an extra copy of everything.

While I was over at Kinko's photocopying I came across a

transcript of the telephone call with me and Dan Traxler. At first I was infuriated. I thought 'Wait a minute, I've already hired a lawyer, how can they tape my phone calls?' I didn't know law enforcement could tape phone calls without your permission. I thought if you had a lawyer they had to go through your lawyer. That's the way civil law works.

As I began reading the transcript, I remembered the conversation. I remember telling Al. I called him up right after the conversation and told him Dan admitted telling me all this again and he said 'Well, it's interesting, but it's still your word against his.'

When I got a copy of the transcript I remember calling Al and telling him 'You remember everything I told you? It's all right here in the transcript.'

Al said 'I'll be darned, it's here. It's here!' It was the DA's efforts to entrap and their efforts to push the envelope and pervert the truth that freed me. During that phone call, Dan Traxler and I had a conversation which became the basis for the dismissal of the indictment by Judge Smith. I recall Judge Smith saying at the hearing: 'If his treasurer tells him it doesn't have to be reported, where is his criminal intent? When the judge asked that question, I was sitting next to Wendy. I just remember squeezing her hand and whispering: 'Finally, somebody gets this! The press was playing it like I was some evil guy. It seemed they wanted to believe the worst.

I was so thrilled that Judge Smith figured it out. And then Judge Smith compared all of Traxler's prior transcripts with what he said to the Grand Jury and essentially called Traxler a liar. I think he said he had 'a creative recollection of events,' a nice way of calling him a liar.

MM: What do you think was the motivation of the DA's Office? Why would they hide certain evidence?

SB: Several things come to mind. The District Attorney had already announced his intention to run for Attorney General of the state of California. Several people told me of personal conversations he had where he said that if he could get a conviction against me, he would be the next Attorney General. Due to the fact that Michael Capizzi always seemed to have success in these cases by way of settlements, plea bargains and resignations, I'm convinced he never thought their conduct before the grand jury would see the light of day. The DA came to me early and offered settlements. They said they were going to indict me and offered to settle the case if I pled guilty to certain charges. I told my lawyer 'No.' at every turn. I didn't do what they were accusing me of and I wasn't going to plead guilty. I really believe that they never thought the transcripts would see the light of day or that I would be able to generate enough financial support to fight the charges. I believe he thought he was just going to extract a plea bargain, perhaps a resignation, put a notch on his belt and look forward to becoming Attorney General. I think that was his whole M.O., but we chose to fight and expose all of his corruption.

MM: At what point did you say 'I'm not taking any deals.'

SB: There were several times I had to say I wasn't going to plead guilty. You always have to have an open mind for resolution. If there were some things I did like take cash. I did it, I didn't know it was wrong. If that's a misdemeanor I could plead to that. I think it was overkill, but early on, even before the indictment I told my lawyer 'I didn't do this. I'm not going to plead guilty to something I didn't do. I'll let a jury put me in prison before I'd do that.'

On October 9, 1996, right before my wedding, Wendy and I went through all the charges and she said 'Did you do that?' I said 'I didn't do that.' She asked 'Did you do that?' I said 'Well, I did this.' She asked 'Did you know it was wrong?' 'No, I didn't'. She knew that she had made the deposit in my account. She knew I had nothing to do with that.

MM: Your wife?

SB: Yes. Wendy knew I had nothing to do with those three counts. Two felonies and a misdemeanor. She said 'That's just ridiculous, you would never plead to that.' We jointly made a decision to fight the charges and never plead guilty to something I didn't do. She said that would be fundamentally dishonest. 'You cannot go before a judge and declare something that's dishonest by pleading guilty to these things.'

MM: How did you pay your legal fees?

SB: Throughout the four years I retained five different lawyers to deal with various issues. My legal bills exceeded $350,000 Some of it came from my savings, but the bulk of it came from friends and supporters who were permitted to contribute to my campaign account. There were many times when I didn't know where the money was going to come from and I think that's part of the DA's strategy. But every time I needed funds, the Good Lord provided.

MM: Did you ever think maybe it's just not worth it?

SB: Once we made the decision to fight, Wendy and I never

gave up hope. I never knew how it was going to happen, but I never lost faith. One time I had to come up with $30,000 and I only had $5,000. I had no idea how I was going to get $25,000. I was in Sacramento and I went to church. At the service I ran into Ben Klaffke, a man I'd met two years earlier on the ski slopes in Austria. He'd been reading about my situation in the papers and that same day he wrote me a check for the $25,000. That's when I knew God was watching over me.

MM: How has this ordeal impacted you?

SB: I noted that Republicans traditionally provided a blind endorsement for law enforcement. Generally, Republicans approve every request by law enforcement to draft or change a law to increase their power. The experience I had brought a refreshing change to that process by pointing out that law enforcement is no different than any other bureaucracy. It can become bloated and unresponsive to the needs of the people. It's important that we equip law enforcement with all the tools needed to fight crime, yet at the same time we need to build reasonable safeguards into the system. We need to protect the public against abuse by the few who choose to abuse the power entrusted to them.

END OF INTERVIEW

The Ruling of Judge Smith

After months of motions and mountains of paperwork, Judge James Smith dismissed counts 1 thru 17 of the indictment. Counts 18 thru 22, which were not dismissed, were not re-filed.

NON-STATUTORY MOTION TO DISMISS

Johnson places upon the prosecution the burden of presenting to the grand jury exculpatory evidence in their possession. Williams does not abrogate Johnson in California. (Commiskey and Penal Code Section 939.7)

As to Defendant Baugh it is clear that the viability Counts 1-17 of the Indictment rest upon the testimony of David Traxler. That is not to say there was no other relevant evidence adduced during the proceedings, but without Mr. Traxler's testimony there is little doubt the indictment would not survive a motion to dismiss pursuant to Penal Code Section 995 as to some if not all of these counts. To characterize Mr. Traxler as being evasive and ambivalent in his statements made to investigators employed by the District Attorney prior to his grand jury testimony would be an understatement. Although one of these inconsistencies, his several versions of who signed one of the reports submitted to the Fair Political Practices Commission, was pointed out to the Grand Jury, this revelation merely scratched the surface of Mr. Traxler's apparent creative recollection of the events regarding which he testified. It is arguable that as a result of these prehearing interviews the prosecution was able to refine out the many mistakes, misstatements, and faulty recollections so that when appearing before the Grand Jury Mr. Traxler offered only truthful testimony. While this may be argued it begs the question. The Grand Jury, being the trier of the fact, is charged with determining the credibility of witnesses testifying before it and the truthfulness of the testimony offered. In performing this function it may consider prior inconsistent statements of witnesses, especially when such statements are clearly exculpatory in nature. Defendant's Reply To Opposition To Motion To Dismiss Indictment provides an excellent exposition of Mr. Traxler's testimony before the Grand Jury and prior statements made by him that were known to prosecution and not presented to the Grand Jury. The viability of Counts 1-17 is so clearly dependent upon the testimony of Mr. Traxler that to have deprived the Grand Jury of the opportunity to fully evaluate his credibility and consider prior statements that were both inconsistent and exculpatory as to the Defendant is fatal to the People's position. This aversion on the part of the prosecution to the use of prior inconsistent statements appears to have been limited only to those that were exculpatory in nature. On many occasions witnesses who testified contrary to the People's position were "impeached" with prior statements that were more supportive of that position, while prior statements that were exculpatory were withheld.

Counts 1-17 of the Indictment are ordered dismissed.

Counts 18-22 of the Indictment relate to various items alleged to have not been properly reported on Statements of Economic Interest filed by the Defendant. The Johnson arguments offered by counsel for Defendant in support of their motion to dismiss these counts are similar in nature to those submitted in regard to Counts 1-17. However, the exculpatory evidence relating to Counts 18-22 alleged to have been withheld by the People is largely circumstantial and not as clearly erosive of the inculpatory evidence presented. Although speculation as to the effect the presentation of such evidence would have had on the Grand Jury's deliberations is dangerous, the Court finds that there does not exist a substantial possibility that the outcome of those deliberations would have been different as to Counts 18-22 had the additional evidence been offered.

Defendants Motion to Dismiss Counts 18-22 is denied.

The Defense

Allan H. Stokke was born on a farm in North Dakota and came to California in 1965. He wanted to be "far away from winter weather" and settled in Orange County, where he went to work for the district attorney's office.

After working as a prosecutor for three years Stokke decided to go into private practice and is now a highly respected criminal law specialist and trial attorney. In a recent interview, Stokke shared his thoughts about the Baugh case:

MM: "When you were a prosecutor did you work on any particular projects which investigated corruption?

AS: Yes, I did some work in special assignments, some of which involved political corruption and judicial corruption.

MM: So Orange County has always had a special unit to investigate political and judicial corruption?

AS: I think it was created while I was there and until recently they've always had a special unit that focused on that kind of thing. The present district attorney has made changes and there's no longer a Special Assignments Unit.

MM: We recently saw several political prosecutions which may have been done in a hurry and for political gain. Do you think over the years that former District Attorney Michael Capizzi formed a team that specialized in political corruption so that could be his claim to fame?

AS: He clearly had more of an emphasis on that sort of thing than any prior district attorney did and my impression is that it was more than in other counties. It did seem that's what his reputation was all about. I can't say he intended it to be that way, but it certainly was that way.

MM: Would you say he made it tough to be corrupt in Orange County?

AS: You could say that, but he also made it tough for some other politicians who weren't intending to be corrupt, but who may have stepped over the line in technical matters that weren't necessarily appropriate to be handled in the criminal justice system. Many indiscretions or lapses in judgment are handled by other counties as administrative violations or not handled at all. In this county, because of the machinery that existed and the desire on Mr. Capizzi's part to handle them, minor violations became criminal prosecutions.

MM: To the average newspaper reader and TV viewer, Mr. Capizzi could certainly be given great plaudits for saving the taxpayers from the fraudulent practices of corrupt politicians. However, do you think it's possible that when he decided to run for Attorney General, he realized he was going to need a major amount of publicity? Do you think he decided a couple of major investigations or indictments could help him get elected?

AS: I've thought long and hard about that question. Any politician running for statewide office needs as much public exposure as he can get. I looked at all the possible reasons that may have caused some of the actions which took place here and I can't think of any other reason. Nothing else seems logical for the very extreme actions which took place here involving Grand Jury abuse and other lapses in judgment on the part of that office. It wasn't being done by other people in the office. Mr.

Capizzi was very closely involved with these prosecutions.

MM: Is it possible he didn't have enough control over those in his office who may have pushed the envelope in this case?

AS: No. He had too much control. The major criticism for years has been that deputies were never given discretion to do things on their own. Things were always done with the approval of superiors at very high levels. In this particular case, I know that Mr. Capizzi was very closely involved in it because I had conversations with him during the course of the prosecution. I believe there was testimony that the deputy DA's appearing in court spoke with him and kept him up to date on a regular basis all during the investigation and prosecution of Scott Baugh.

MM: I recently interviewed Assemblyman Baugh and he described, sometimes very emotionally, some of the things that happened to him. Could you give me a thumbnail sketch of what you saw when you became involved and how this case developed?

AS: There were DA investigators scurrying all over the place interviewing people and Scott Baugh wanted to know what he should be doing. That was several days before the recall election of Doris Allen. He won that election and we went from there to the primary which came about in March 1996. The old grand jury finished in 1995 and we went on March 1996 with the new grand jury which had been sworn in on January 1, 1996. All during that time, Scott Baugh was very, very concerned. There was a tremendous amount of pressure on him. During that time he was I believe improperly searched, at least it was improper in the way it was done.

MM: That was the search of his house?

AS: Yes. And the timing of it was very questionable, as well as the abuse he was subjected to at the time because of his use of a camera. I couldn't imagine why they wouldn't allow photographs to be taken. They shouldn't have had anything to hide. It didn't seem to make a lot of sense. It was during that period of time that they appeared to be moving very quickly and they did eventually indict him about five days before the March primary.

MM: Do you think there was any intent in the DA's office to file that before the primary?

AS: I think timing had to have been a factor. There were red flags all over. Red flags which normally cause an experienced prosecutor to hold back. Guy Ormes was the man most out in front at that point in time and there were red flags that he or John Anderson, who worked with him, should have said 'Whoa, let's resolve some of these discrepancy problems between Traxler's various statements. Let's take a close, hard look at this.' Instead, they kept Traxler's 95% inconsistent statements away from the Grand Jury. A very unusual action. So timing had to have been important and they later said they were in touch with the District Attorney all through that period of time. I can only conclude that they were being pressed hard to get the indictment done before the election.

MM: By who?

AS: By Mr. Capizzi. They both said later on that they kept him up to date during that period of time.

MM: When Scott Baugh was elected, he got more votes than the other candidates, but why did he have to run again three months later?

AS: He won the seat outright in late November of '95 because it was a recall election and different rules apply. In March he was running as an incumbent, but he still had a primary to go through and there were other Republicans opposing him.

MM: Did you ever discover a relationship between any of those opponents and the DA's office?

AS: In the 1996 election, Haydee Tillotson did not run, but she did run in the 1998 election and she had a very definite connection with Mike Capizzi at that point in time.

MM: What connection was that?

AS: She was on his campaign finance committee. She contributed money to Mr. Capizzi when he was running for Attorney General. Her husband contributed money and her campaign manager, Mr Laird, and his family contributed large sums of money to Mr. Capizzi. So it was to their benefit, to Haydee Tillotson's benefit and to Mr. Laird's benefit that Mr. Baugh be prosecuted. If he were prosecuted, convicted and sent to prison, he would be out of the way and Haydee Tillotson would likely be the winner. Our argument all during the course of the recusal motion that that's a very improper connection and the impartial prosecutor had disappeared at some point in time and was now partial.

MM: How did you find out about this connection?

AS: The contributions were reported in their campaign finance reports. We also did subpoenas which disclosed her position on Capizzi's finance committee.

MM: Was there ever a time when anyone in the DA's office indicated to you that they did not agree with what was happening?

AS: There were a substantial number of deputy DA's who privately spoke about their lack of support for the prosecution. I understand that Capizzi had spread the word within the office that the Baugh case was the most important case in the office. This seemed rather astounding to many people within and without the DA's office. That death penalty cases would be considered less important than this, which many people considered a misdemeanor case, caused some concern.

MM: Scott Baugh told me that he had been told privately that Capizzi had said to several people that if he could get a conviction of Scott Baugh, he would be assured of winning the election for Attorney General. Are you aware of those comments?

AS: I did not hear any of those statements myself. I've heard that information, but I didn't hear that from anyone in the DA's office.

MM: There's a particular moment in the investigation which Scott Baugh described very candidly. He said he went to pick up a box of transcripts during the discovery process and while he was standing at Kinko's making copies, he found a transcript of a phone call with Dan Traxler that he didn't know was taped. He talked to me about conversations he had with you before and after that transcript was found. Do you recall that transcript?

AS: Yes, I do. Scott had been telling me that his conversations with Traxler were different from what Traxler was testifying to

MM: But that's unbelievable! How could the DA not present that to the Grand Jury? How could they do that?

AS: I think that's the reason Judge Smith made such an unusual ruling. He dismissed the case because the District Attorney kept this evidence from the Grand Jury. That and a substantial number of other statements which were also not given to the Grand Jury.

MM: Does it appear to you that the modus operandi of the DA's office over the years had become to investigate, indict, overcharge and then extract some kind of settlement?

AS: We've seen that happen in a number of situations. I think there certainly was overcharging taking place in Scott Baugh's case. I can't imagine anybody trying to prosecute that as a felony. The DA did eventually offer a plea to a lesser charge, so that could have been the District Attorney's theory here in making the heavy charges. It's possible.

MM: I've heard it said that a DA's office throws a lot of charges against the wall to see what sticks. However, in this case with the political ramifications, is it possible that the DA decided to charge acts that were not criminal and intentionally include them so the target of the investigation would take a deal instead of fighting the charges?

AS: No question about it.

MM: Do you think spending so much time and effort prosecuting Scott Baugh had a negative impact on the DA's office's ability to prosecute other crimes?

Conflict of Interest Ruling

Defense attorney Stokke argued repeatedly that the DA had a conflict of interest and the case against Scott Baugh should never have been investigated by his office. In 1999, Superior Court Judge Francisco Briseno agreed:

SUPERIOR COURT OF THE STATE OF CALIFORNIA FOR THE COUNTY OF ORANGE

MINUTE ORDER

Department _____40_____

Court convened at__________A.M.____________________ present

Hon.__FRANCISCO P. BRISEÑO__, Judge; ______________, Deputy Clerk;

________________, Deputy Marshal;________________Reporter;

and the following proceedings were had:

PEOPLE OF THE STATE OF CALIFORNIA v. SCOTT R. BAUGH
CASE NO. 96 CF2840

Minute Order Ruling on defense motion to disqualify the Orange County District Attorney from acting as the prosecuting attorney on this case.

ALLAN STOKKE	Counsel for defendant
WILLIAM J. KOPENY	Counsel for defendant
JOHN CONLEY	Counsel for plaintiff
CRAIG McKINNON	Counsel for plaintiff
PAMELA A. RATNER	Deputy Attorney General

Summary of Case

The current charges arise from alleged activity engaged in by Scott Baugh when he was a candidate for the 67th Assembly District. Between September 21, 1995 and November 28, 1995, a special recall election was held in the 67th Assembly District. Several persons filed to run including Scott Baugh, Haydee Tillotson, Laurie Campbell, and Linda Moulton Patterson, among others. The election was held November 28, 1995 and Scott Baugh was elected. A recall election does not have a Primary and the candidate with the greatest plurality wins. The recall portion dealt with Doris Allen, who was recalled on that same election, and since Baugh was successful he simply filled in for the remainder of her term. In March of 1996 Baugh had to stand for election again. In other words, on March 26,

PEOPLE OF THE STATE OF CALIFORNIA v. SCOTT R. BAUGH
CASE NO. 96 CF2840
Page 2 of 10

1996, a Primary election was conducted for the 67th Assembly District in which Baugh was a candidate. (It is noted that Tillotson was not a candidate in March, 1996) Baugh was reelected in 1996. This Assembly Seat was up for election again this year and Baugh was challenged by Tillotson and others during this campaign with Baugh prevailing.

Haydee Tillotson, as noted above, was a substantial candidate for the 67th Assembly District in both the recall election of 1995 and during this year's election effort. She raised over $167,000 during the 1995 election (mostly, if not all, loans to herself) and she was very active during this year's efforts both on the financial aspect as well as seeking to publicize the charges pending against Baugh through campaign statements, mailers and candidate statement sent to registered voters.

The District Attorney, seeking to become California Attorney General, commenced his state campaign some time in 1996. During this hearing it was disclosed for the first time that Haydee Tillotson's husband had contributed $500 to Michael Capizzi for his campaign fund for Attorney General. Haydee Tillotson also contributed $250 to Mr. Capizzi on January 17, 1998. In addition, Haydee Tillotson has been listed on Capizzi's fund raising committees.

The charges filed against Baugh are the result of an investigation initiated by the Orange County District Attorney sometime in October, 1995. The investigation led to the taking of testimony before the Grand Jury in December, 1995. However, the Grand Jury was discharged at the end of December, 1995 and a new Grand Jury was impaneled in January, 1996. The

PEOPLE OF THE STATE OF CALIFORNIA v. SCOTT R. BAUGH
CASE NO. 96 CF2840
Page 3 of 10

new Grand Jury heard testimony in February and early March of 1996 which resulted in an indictment against Baugh. In September, 1996, counts 1 – 17 were dismissed by Superior Court Judge James L. Smith on Johnson Error by the District Attorney (failure to disclose material statements to the Grand Jurors during their investigation). The District Attorney did not appeal and thereafter dismissed the remaining counts on their own motion and :efiled new charges in October, 1996 in Central Municipal Court which resulted in the current case before this court. Attached to this minute order are copies of the first indictment, the felony complaint and current information.

The charges filed against the defendant arise from his alleged failure to disclose required information in his submitted campaign disclosure statements during the special 67th Assembly District Recall Election September, 1995 through November, 1995.

uling

Motion by defendant to disqualify the Orange County District Attorney and nis office is hereby granted.

A. This court finds that an actual conflict of interest exists between the District Attorney and the defendant, and further finds that the conflict of interest is so substantial as to render it unlikely that the defendant will receive fair treatment throughout the pending proceedings unless the entire District Attorney's Office is removed from the case. It is acceptance of campaign financial contributions by the District Attorney, with knowledge of the fact that Tillotson was not only a current opponent but had been a substantial candidate in the very same recall election as the defendant, that results in the determination that a conflict of interest exists.

Specific findings:

1. The District Attorney, in his campaign efforts to be elected as California's Attorney General in the 1998 election, accepted money from Haydee Tillotson in the amount of $250 on January 17, 1998 and accepted $500 from her husband on December 20, 1996. At the time the District Attorney accepted the money, he knew that Tillotson had been a political opponent of Baugh in the 1995 special recall election.
2. Baugh's campaign disclosures filed during the 1995 special recall election are the basis of the allegations in the current case.
3. Haydee Tillotson was a substantial candidate in the special recall election, in that she had raised the sum of over $167,000 in a very short period of time (September 21, 1995 to November, 1995).
4. Haydee Tillotson was also a candidate against Baugh for the 67th Assembly District in this year's election.
5. Haydee Tillotson is on the host committee for a fund raising event for the District Attorney's campaign efforts for the Attorney General Office.

PEOPLE OF THE STATE OF CALIFORNIA v. SCOTT R. BAUGH
CASE NO. 96 CF2840
Page 5 of 10

6. The District Attorney has referred specifically to the 1995 election opponents of Baugh as being disadvantaged by the defendant's failure to make proper financial disclosures, in the District Attorney's public statements concerning the purpose of his prosecution of this case.
7. Tillotson has referred to the current case against Baugh in seeking political advantage in the 1998 election for the 67th Assembly District.
8. The fact that Tillotson and Capizzi were not successful in their respective campaigns does not moot the conflict of interest.

B. The court's determination that the conflict is so substantial that the defendant will not receive fair treatment is based on the following major considerations.
1. The finding of misconduct by Judge James L. Smith in September, 1996 that the District Attorney did not disclose all material evidence to the Grand Jury during the hearings that resulted in the indictment.
2. Review of the underlying circumstances that led to Johnson Error reflect adversely on the District Attorney's ability to be fair in the processing of the current case.

In reviewing the events leading up to how Daniel Traxler was presented to the Grand Jury it is clear that the only reason for rushing Mr. Traxler before the Grand Jury on March 1 and 5, 1995 was to seek an indictment prior to the scheduled primary election in March, 1996 for the

PEOPLE OF THE STATE OF CALIFORNIA v. SCOTT R. BAUGH
CASE NO. 96 CF2840
Page 6 of 10

67th Assembly District. The District Attorney's office interviewed Traxler eight different times between November, 1995 and March 1, 1996. The District Attorney Investigator states that as of the interview of March 1, 1996 he felt that Traxler was not being consistent. This interview takes place on the day Traxler is called before the Grand Jury. Mr. Traxler was Baugh's campaign treasurer during the 1995 special recall election. He signed the very same campaign disclosure statements that the defendant signed that are the basis for the current charges. Mr. Traxler is also authorized to sign checks for the Bank of America bank account created for "Baugh for Assembly account". It is alleged irregularities between Baugh's personal banking account (Wells Fargo), the "Baugh for Assembly account" (Bank of America), and the campaign disclosure statements filed by Traxler and the defendant that give rise to the current proceedings.

Obviously, Traxler was identified as being an essential person to interview and between November 21, 1995 and March 1, 1996 Investigator Sorley interviewed Traxler eight times. On the last interview of March 1, 1996 Sorley noted some changes in Traxler's statements. Traxler's testimony was taken before the Grand Jury on March 1 and 5, 1996. The Grand Jury was not advised of Traxler's prior statements that were inconsistent with his Grand Jury testimony. This failure to advise or inform led to Johnson Error. In order to evaluate whether the District Attorney will exercise his discretion in an evenhanded manner it is important to discuss what is significant as it regards this event.

Guy Ormes is a seasoned, veteran prosecutor who has an excellent reputation and whose best attribute is that he is meticulous. Mr. Ormes

PEOPLE OF THE STATE OF CALIFORNIA v. SCOTT R. BAUGH
CASE NO. 96 CF2840
Page 7 of 10

always talks to his investigators, his witnesses, and reviews all his witness's statements before calling a witness to testify. Mr. Ormes is not sloppy. I accept his declaration that he was unaware of the March 1, 1996 statement by Traxler to the District Attorney Investigator. But, that statement indicates what Judge Evans noted, that the prosecutors were rushing things before the Grand Jury. Since the Grand Jury had just been impaneled in January, 1996 there was no need to rush. The only reasonable conclusion is that the District Attorney was seeking to get a return of the indictment by the time of the March 25, 1996 Primary. The District Attorney has discretion as to what to investigate, what witnesses to call, what charges to file, and who to charge. In this case they did not carefully review the statements of a key material witness, they did not disclose prior inconsistent statements of the campaign treasurer to the Grand Jury, and it is noted they have not filed any charges against Traxler even though he signed some of the basic documents that are the basis of the current charges against Baugh.

Mr. Traxler is a major, if not key witness, in the current case. As treasurer, he had day-to-day contact with the defendant. He was responsible for the proper accounting documents related to the 1995 election. His credibility, recollection, and accuracy can reasonably be anticipated to be a prime consideration in the evaluation of this case at all stages of the proceeding. The Johnson Error is not simply a past deed.

Both Deputy District Attorneys presenting the case to the Grand Jury indicate they kept the District Attorney aware of the status of the investigation, of the Grand Jury proceedings, from which, the inference is

PEOPLE OF THE STATE OF CALIFORNIA v. SCOTT R. BAUGH
CASE NO. 96 CF2840
Page 8 of 10

drawn that the District Attorney was aware of identities of the persons who were candidates for the 67th Assembly District during the 1995 special recall election (i.e., Haydee Tillotson was a political opponent of the defendant).

For the record it is noted that Traxler was interviewed by the District Attorney on 11/21/95, 11/22/95, 12/1/95, 12/12/95, 12/14/95, 12/19/95, 1/18/96 and 3/1/96.

Mr. Traxler testified before the Grand Jury on 3/1/96 and 3/5/96. The indictment was returned on 3/21/96. The Primary election 3/25/96. The Grand Jury that heard Traxler was impaneled January, 1996. The indictment consisted of 22 counts; 5 felonies and 17 misdemeanors.

Superior Court Judge James L. Smith, on September 19, 1996 dismissed counts 1 - 17 on Johnson Error. The District Attorney did not appeal. The District Attorney refiled new charges on October 9, 1996 in Central Municipal Court. The new complaint alleged 18 counts; 5 felonies and 13 misdemeanors. In December, 1997 the preliminary hearing magistrate dismissed 3 felonies and 3 misdemeanors. The new information alleges violation of the law dealing with bank records or campaign statements signed by Traxler.

Change of Circumstances

Any judge views a previously heard motion with skepticism, but both parties have agreed that Judge Evans was not advised of the relationship between Tillotson and the District Attorney during his hearing on the motion to disqualify the District Attorney heard April, 1997, therefore, this court has granted the defense's request for the present hearing.

PEOPLE OF THE STATE OF CALIFORNIA v. SCOTT R. BAUGH
CASE NO. 96 CF2840
Page 9 of 10

This court has reviewed for the purposes of this motion the declarations and evidence presented during this hearing. Pursuant to the joint request of both parties, this court has taken judicial notice under E.C. 452(d) and 453 of the court file Case No. 96 CF2840, the prior indictment as to this defendant, Case No. 96 ZF0020, and the Writ filed by defendant, Case No. 77-80-29, including exhibits submitted by the parties. The court has reviewed the preliminary hearing and exhibits introduced in this case.

It is the joint finding:

1. Acceptance of money from a political opponent of defendant by the District Attorney, with knowledge that Tillotson was a candidate in the 1995 special recall election,

   and

2. Judge Smith's finding of misconduct

   that

compels the finding by this court that a conflict of interest actually exists that meets the level set forth in section 1424 of the Penal Code and mandates the disqualification of the District Attorney from further prosecution of this case.

It would be prudent to set forth what is not the basis of the court's findings. They are as follows:

1. Personal animosity between defendant and District Attorney, if any.
2. Political differences within the Republican Party, if any.

PEOPLE OF THE STATE OF CALIFORNIA v. SCOTT R. BAUGH
CASE NO. 96 CF2840
Page 10 of 10

3. The District Attorney's seeking to be elected Attorney General for the State.
4. The District Attorney's reference in his political campaign to his career earned reputation as being tough on political corruption.
5. The episode between the District Attorney and Judge Smith reference a prior investigation of the Orange Unified School District on October 9, 1996.
6. The hearing between Judge Carter and the District Attorney on February 26, 1997.
7. The Hearing of February 14, 1997 before Judge Marjorie Carter wherein Assistant District Attorney Romney sought to recuse Central Municipal Court judges.

In making this determination I have accepted the People's understanding of the key applicable legal concepts. I simply did not agree that Tillotson was just another private citizen making a political contribution, nor do I dismiss the importance of the finding of Johnson Error as it pertains to this particular case. I do agree that a motion under section 1424 set a high standard of proof; in my twenty-one years on the Bench this will be the second such motion granted. I also agree that an elected public official should not be treated any differently than any other accused person.

DATED:____________________________

Case Closed

Daniel Traxler signed a confession taking responsibility for the reporting errors, however under state law, the candidate and the treasurer are jointly liable for any and all mistakes. On July 27, 1999, Traxler and Assemblyman Baugh agreed to pay a fine of $48,700 and the case was closed.

A Silver Lining

Could you defend yourself against a prosecutor with unlimited resources and a political agenda? During his four years in office, Assemblyman Baugh, who now serves as Assembly Republican Leader, has introduced several bills which place more safeguards in our justice system.

Baugh recalled that in the case against him, DA Capizzi, "in a display of bureaucratic arrogance" argued that he was not required to disclose exculpatory evidence. In 1997, Baugh introduced a measure which requires prosecutors to disclose exculpatory evidence to a grand jury. This measure was passed by the Assembly and Senate and is now state law.

Another Baugh measure which has passed the Assembly and Senate seeks to allow targets of grand jury investigations to have their lawyers with them. "The government can have a team of lawyers trained in the art of interrogation." Baugh said, "But you have to go in alone. That's nonsense." This bill will become law if and when it is signed by newly elected Governor Gray Davis, a Democrat.

Four years ago corporate lawyer Scott Baugh had an interest in entering national politics. He can't run for the Assembly again due to term limits, but hopefully, politics is in his future.

When we were reviewing the transcript of the interview for accuracy, Baugh told me he hopes one day to serve in Congress. If he does decide to be a candidate for national office, I think an important part of his message will include what he said to me as I was leaving:

"If prosecutors are not restrained by safeguards, they'll be able to indict a ham sandwich for murder!"

* * *

The Candidates

6

The Reserve Officer

Chuck Carter is a friendly guy with an infectious laugh who manages to fit in wherever he happens to be. A successful businessman, for 22 years he worked without pay for the Orange County Sheriff's Department and several police departments. His work with Anaheim Vice was instrumental in helping them shut down the largest bookmaking operation in Orange County history.

In 1994, Captain Andy Romero of the Orange County Sheriff's Department was hired as the Chief of Police in Bell Gardens. Located in Southern Los Angeles County, Bell Gardens is a predominantly Hispanic community where blue collar workers live and raise their families. It is also the home of The Bicycle Club, an extremely successful casino which offers Asian gambling.

Soon after he took over, Chief Romero received reports of drug dealing and corruption at the casino. Remembering the good work Chuck Carter had done in the past, Chief Romero asked him to come to work at Bell Gardens. Neither man had any idea what they were getting themselves into.

Welcome to Uncle Sam's Casino

In 1981, businessman George Hardie approached the City of Bell Gardens with plans to build a card club. He formed Park Place Associates, Ltd. with 35 investors and in 1984 made a deal with builder Sam Gilbert. In exchange for a 65% interest, Gilbert agreed to build the club and formed CGL Corporation with his son, Michael.

After the Bicycle Club had been built, Gilbert and his associates, Barry Kramer and Jerome Kramer, were indicted for smuggling $500,000. worth of marijuana and laundering $11 million through CGL Corporation.

A minority share of the casino was seized under the Asset Forfeiture Program following an investigation and prosecution by the US Attorney in Florida. The United States Marshall's Office in Los Angeles was charged with overseeing the 30% interest owned by the government.

The Trustee in charge of collecting this money was reportedly paid $30,000 per month, so needless to say, business was good.

United States Senate - Washington D.C. - March 1996

Chuck Carter didn't know that the Bicycle Club had been the subject of an extensive investigation by the United States Senate Sub Committee charged with overseeing the Asset Forfeiture Program. At a hearing in March of 1996, former Director of Security at the Bicycle Club, Douglas Sparkes, described the Bicycle Club as the "Macau of the West" and testified about money laundering, tip skimming and narcotics trafficking. Carter also didn't know that Sparkes sued Freeman for forcibly removing him from his position and ending his career.

In 1992, business was booming at The Bicycle Club. With 1800 employees, the casino accounted for about 80% of the revenue of Bell Gardens. Doug Sparkes, son of the former police chief of Buena Park, California, had spent his entire life enforcing the law. Retired after 20 years with the Los Angeles Sheriff's Department, he was working as a private investigator when he served a subpoena for records on the Bicycle Club. Then-manager John Sutton mentioned they were looking for a Director of their 80 man security department. Sparkes left his card and a few days later he got a call to meet with George Hardie, who hired him on the spot.

Working with Police Chief Andy Romero, Sparkes cooperated with state and federal law enforcement on a regular basis. His main contact was the Office of California Attorney General Dan Lundgren.

In 1996, Lundgren reported to Washington that extensive evidence of organized criminal activity had been uncovered at the Bicycle Club/. In February 1996 Sparkes was subpoenaed to testify before the Senate Sub Committee which oversees the Asset Forfeiture Program. This hearing was opened with a statement by the committee Chairman, Senator Roth:

> "This is a sad story in our long history of uncovering waste fraud and mismanagement in government programs. The Sub Committee has discovered that as incredible as it sounds, the United States Marshall Service is running a gambling casino and has been doing so for nearly six years. However, this is not just any gambling casino. The Marshals run the infamous Bicycle Club Casino in Bell Gardens, California. The Bicycle Club is no stranger to this Sub Committee. During hearings the Sub Committee held in 1991 on Asian organized crime, law enforcement officials testified that the Bicycle Club was suspected of being a money laundering center and that the casino's Asian games manager was suspected of hiring gang members to work there. The Marshals ran the casino even then. Today, we will focus on

this particular situation as a case study of the problems plaguing the Asset Forfeiture Program."

END OF EXCERPT

When called to testify, Sparkes provided the committee with an overview of the problems he faced at the Bicycle Club:

"I have been the Director of Security at the Bicycle Club Casino since June 1992, when I was hired by George Hardie, then General Manager of the club. As the Director of Security for the club, my duties include maintaining proper staff, designing and recommending procedures for greater protection of the club, employees and company assets. I am also responsible for being the liaison with all law enforcement and governmental agencies and security related associations.

From the standpoint of law enforcement, the club is seen as a place where crime is permitted and condoned. The club has a worldwide reputation as the Macau of the West, where it is understood that the management will tolerate almost anything as long as the management profits from the activity and will continue to profit from the activity."

END OF EXCERPT

While all of this was going on, Andy Romero left Bell Gardens and is now the Chief of Police in the city of Orange. He was replaced by Sergeant Fred Freeman.

Shortly after Sparkes returned to California, Chief Freeman wrote a letter instructing him to "cease and desist" all investigations. When Sparkes contacted the Attorney General's Office, they said Freeman had no right to tell him what to do. A few weeks later Sparkes was escorted off the casino property by three Bell Gardens police officers in RAID jackets. After he was out, they seized his personal papers, tax information, notebooks, computer files and portions of a book he was writing. All this was done without a search warrant.

A few days later, Attorney General Lundgren overrode the Bell Gardens Police Department and suspended the licenses of all the people Sparkes had been investigating. Chief Freeman retaliated by suspending Sparkes' work permit and refusing to hold a hearing within seven days as required.

Sparkes has filed a lawsuit against Chief Freeman and the City of Bell Gardens in LA Federal Court which is pending at the present time.

Background

In 1994, Chief Romero wanted Carter to "fit in" at the Bicycle Club by playing the part of a high roller. Pursuant to policy, a background investigation was conducted by then-Sergeant Fred Freeman. Carter was hired by the City of Bell Gardens as a reserve officer and immediately began his undercover work.

In no time at all, Chuck Carter became a familiar face at the Bicycle Club. Using a car leased for him by the police department, he met dealers, doormen, cashiers, pit bosses and "runners", all the while gathering information and filing reports. Not an experienced gambler, he made his usual bankroll of $500. last as long as possible as he gathered information about private dinners and parties given at little or no charge for city council members. Soon he was learning about large amounts of cash being laundered through the casino by convicted felons.

After Carter reported drug dealing and organized criminal activity, Chief Romero invited other agencies to participate. The Los Angeles Sheriff's Department assigned their highly specialized organized crime detail to work with Carter and things began to get serious. With the larger and well financed Sheriff's unit involved, plans came together for joint contributions of time and resources.

Plans were made and money was spent to organize a cooperative effort. Before long Carter was invited to launder money through the casino. Preparations were under way, but Chief Romero left the department and Freeman had not yet been briefed on the operation.

Sharon Leslie, former secretary to Chief Freeman, testified that shortly after he learned Chuck Carter was working undercover at the casino, she overheard Chief Freeman on the phone talking to a city council member about it. Afraid for Chuck's safety, she called Carter on his cell phone to tell him what she'd just heard Freeman do. A politician now knew Chuck was in the casino. His cover was blown. As of that moment, the operation was over.

The Anaheim Police Department wanted Chuck Carter to return to work with them, but during their background search, Chief Freeman falsely told them Carter had ties to organized crime. Where Freeman obtained this information is a mystery, especially since he had conducted the background check when Carter was hired by Bell Gardens.

Anaheim PD then contacted Los Alamitos Police Chief Mike Skogh, who said Carter did not have a clear record. None of Carter's former supervisors at Los Alamitos PD knew anything about the Skogh statement and have signed sworn declarations. Stating that Carter was an excellent officer. Shogh and Freeman presented no evidence to back up these allegations, but that didn't seem to matter.

Even with a letter of commendation from the Anaheim Chief of Police, the late Randy Gaston, Carter could not be hired by Anaheim PD.

Chuck Carter's dream of working as a security consultant in his retirement had been undermined by two men he hardly even knew. His many friends and associates in law enforcement felt Freeman and Skogh should be required to prove their allegations.

Carter hired attorney Bradley Gage to file a lawsuit which

provides a unique look inside an undercover operation gone wrong.

Accountability Time

Woodland Hills Attorney Bradley Gage, a partner in the law firm of Goldberg & Gage, has filed 18 lawsuits against Chief Freeman and the City of Bell Gardens since September of 1997. In a recent interview, Gage provided an overview:

"Chief Fred Freeman's conduct has resulted in more than $1 million in legal fees to the taxpayers of Bell Gardens. My objective in this lawsuit is to clear Chuck Carter's name, allow him to return to work in law enforcement and to compensate him for emotional and financial losses caused by Freeman's conduct."

According to the *Los Angeles Daily Journal,* three of Mr. Gage's clients have already settled their cases for several hundred thousand dollars plus lifetime pension benefits estimated to be worth more than $1 million..

Gage has strong personal feelings about the situation in Bell Gardens:

"Goldberg & Gage has been involved in the representation of police officers for more than 12 years and we have never seen a case in which so many police officers in one department make such serious allegations of misconduct against their chief. Police chiefs are vested with the public trust and we expect them to uphold the law and treat people fairly."

"Chief Freeman is accused of racism, discrimination and retaliation against police officers who insist that he uphold the law."

Gage's home and office have been broken into and in the

same two week period, the cars of two of his police officer clients have been vandalized. Police reports were filed, but no suspects have been identified. Two other police officer clients were followed after being interviewed by a Fox TV News reporter. In his sworn deposition, Chief Freeman testified that he is the only person authorized to order surveillance of Bell Gardens police officers.

In August 1999, Carter noticed he was being followed on the freeway and recognized the driver as Fred Freeman. The car was registered to the Bell Gardens Police Department and had been assigned to Fred Freeman.

Shortly after Officer Richard Santoro stated in a televised interview that Chief Freeman had made racist statements about Hispanics, he was told by BGPD Commander Eli Magdaleno that he would not receive his retirement badge.

How About Lunch?

According to several BGPD officers, Chief Fred Freeman lived far beyond his means. He filed a personal bankruptcy petition in July of 1994 and his debts were discharged in December of that year, but in 1995 he had new debts. Chief Freeman's former secretary, Sharon Leslie, testified that bill collectors often called the police department seeking payments on delinquent loans.

In October of 1998, I sent Freedom of Information letters to the City of Bell Gardens and the City of Los Alamitos requesting photocopies of all credit card purchases billed to these cities by their police departments.

Los Alamitos responded within a few days with a photocopy of a single purchase of radio equipment made by Chief Skogh. The response from Bell Gardens was another story. After three weeks, I drove to Bell Gardens City Hall and spoke with a clerk, who knew about the request before I'd even finished introducing myself. She said my letter had been given to Anil Gandhy, the Finance Director, and he would be handling the matter. He was not available at that time.

After two more weeks, I returned to Bell Gardens City Hall to speak with Mr. Gandhy and again he was unavailable. The same clerk said the documents had to be retrieved from storage. Two weeks later, I returned to Bell Gardens City Hall and met Mr. Gandhy, who was standing with the clerk.

A clearly overworked but cordial Anil Gandhy escorted me to a conference room. He told me he had the records, but needed clearance from the City Manager to release them. He wanted to know why I needed the copies and I smiled a lot , but told him nothing. When he expressed surprise that I was so persistent, I assured him I'd be back until the records were ready to be picked up.

He didn't call, so the next week I returned with translator Dan McIntosh, a bilingual private investigator based in Ensenada, Mexico. We walked directly into Anil Gandhy's private office and he became extremely nervous. He showed us the documents he was waiting for permission to release and asked if he could Fed-Ex them. I said I'd prefer to pick them up. Again he said he'd call. Once more he didn't call.

A few days later, McIntosh and I returned to see Gandhy and it was clear that he was at the end of his rope. He looked like an invisible vice was squeezing his head. His eyes screamed "Please leave me alone!" as he handed me an inch thick pile of photocopies. Page after page of charges. No meeting topics, no names. When I asked several officers if they'd ever been to a staff meeting at a restaurant, they laughed.

Credit card statements in hand, I met with Sharon Leslie. She'd worked for Chief Freeman only a short time when allegations of racism were filed against Freeman by several minority officers. Shortly after she signed a declaration in support of one of these officers, she was transferred to a basement office in the gaming department. She hired attorney

Bradley Gage, who sued the city. After her deposition was taken, they settled the case quickly.

Several officers I interviewed complained loud and long about problems in the department. Many have lawsuits pending that paint an ugly picture. Did they know that Chuck Carter was working undercover ? No. Did they want to know? No. They just wanted to do their jobs and not have to worry about being transferred or fired by Chief Freeman.

Sharon Leslie had first hand knowledge of what happened at the Bell Gardens Police Department. She reviewed the credit card statements and recalled that Chief Freeman would look for someone to take to lunch so he could use the city credit card and say it was business. "Usually it was Greg Shepherd, his assistant, because no one else was around.", she recalled.

She recalled that every time Chief Freeman went on a trip, he requested per diem expense money before he left, then charged everything on his credit card, which was paid by the city. Why bother to pad your expense account if you can get paid twice?

According to Sharon Leslie, Chief Freeman had used the credit card once to go shopping at Nordstrom's, but reimbursed the city when the bill came in. The December 1996 credit card statement had not been provided and Sharon Leslie gave her opinion as to the reason:

"He went to Nordstrom's in December 1996 and bought a $500. gift certificate using his city credit card. He only shops at Nordstrom's. I think he went Christmas shopping using the gift certificate so the city wouldn't know what he'd bought.

When the bill came in he refused to give it to me. He made a couple of small payments on it, but then I was transferred, so I don't know when or if he paid it."

On January 14, 1999, the deposition of Sharon Leslie was taken and she was questioned about one of the other lawsuits pending against Chief Freeman:

Q: “What city policies did he (Freeman) change for himself?

A: Expense reports. He was the only department manager that didn’t have to fill out an expense report. It was city policy that whenever they went anywhere they had to turn in a complete listing of their expenses, which he did not do.

Q: So then how would he get reimbursed if he didn’t turn in a list, did he just give a total?

A: No, he would ask for money up front and have me prepare paperwork up front. Plus he had a city credit card. And he took the up front money and he charged things on the credit card and he never accounted for anything.

Q: Do you know if he - other than the fact that he didn’t account for anything - ever used the funds or charges improperly?

A: Yes.

Q: Okay, what instances?

A: There were numerous instances.

MR. GAGE: Can you give him some examples? I think that’s what he’s looking for.

A: He would have me do demands for payment for his subsistence pay. If he was traveling where he would receive an amount of money per day for food.

Q: Right. It is per diem.

A: And he would have me make it out for five, six days,

however long he was supposed to be gone. And he would go for two days and he wouldn't return any money to the city. He wouldn't account for it in any way. Or he would take that money and he would go to the conference and he would charge all his meals on the credit card and then the city would pay all the charges for the credit card. And he would not return the per diem money that he received.

Q: Do you have any records of this?

A: No, not personally.

Q: Do you know anyone who does?

A: I'm sure the city has credit card bills. Payments. They should. And when I would try to fill out an expense report— the first couple times that he did this I generated an expense report and he refused to sign it. And I told him that he had to sign one. And he went to City Hall and came back and said that the finance department told him that he did not have to do that.

MR. GAGE: That's something that all prior chiefs had done?

A: Yes.

Q: Okay. Any other instances where you recall this occurring?

A: He would use his city credit card for personal items.

Q: Like what?

A: The City Manager took away the city credit cards from all the department heads, but he got to keep his in order to hold hotel reservations for when he had to travel. But he was not to use it.

Q: Okay.

A: However, there was a personal charge on it to Nordstrom's for $500 that was not authorized by the city. And that when I received the bill I made out the demand for payment and he would not sign it and about another bill came in that was still on there. And probably the third bill that came in showed a small payment of maybe $20. And it was the city's policy to pay the bill in full every month. So I could only assume that he started to pay it himself.

Q: Okay. Any other instances?

A: When he was an Acting Chief he did not have— he and his wife only had one car between them. And so he contacted a rental car agency through our car repair place, which was Downey Ford. Contacted Enterprise Rentals, got a rental car for— well, he told them it was for the police department so he would get a good rate. And he used this car for his personal use and then he refused to pay the bill for months and months and months. And because he said it was for the police department — Enterprise Rental Car was continually hounding me to pay for his rental car.

Q: Okay. Any other instances?

A: And he finally got a city car when he became Chief and he had a CD player put in it, which was unauthorized. And when Downey Ford billed us for the CD player, it was an amount of money that would have required a purchase order. So he had Linda Chavez call Downey Ford and ask them to break it down into two amounts so that it could go by without a purchase order, and they did that. And we kept preparing the bill to be paid, but he wouldn't send it over. And Downey Ford gave us another invoice and it said CD player on it and he made us contact Downey Ford to change it to electronic equipment. And that bill was outstanding for over a year because he would not put it through because he was never authorized to get that CD player. And I don't know if it ever got paid or not.

Q: Any other instances that you recall?

A: I know that he would use the city credit card at lunch time to purchase lunch and alcohol. The city had a policy for not purchasing alcohol. He would put it on the city credit card.

MR. GAGE: While he was on duty?

A: Yes, while he was on duty.

Q: And this is because you saw the bill, or how do you know?

A: I had been to lunch with him and the lieutenants and Linda Chavez on two different occasions and they all ordered drinks and basically they all—Linda and I did not drink and they all harassed us for not drinking.

Q: Who was present?

A: Chief, Shepherd, Reuter and I don't know if Magdaleno was present or not. I don't recall. He probably was.

Q: Okay. Any other instances?

A.: I know that he would use his city credit card for lunches on a real regular basis. He would try to find somebody at lunch time to go to lunch with so he could write it as a lunch meeting. And I mean he would make a lot of attempts. It wasn't like it was a scheduled meeting. He would make attempts to use it."

END OF EXCERPT

The deposition of Chief Freeman was started, postponed, then rescheduled several times. At one videotaped session, Chief Freeman left abruptly, stating that he was ill because looking at attorney Gage made him sick.

The taxpayers of Bell Gardens may have a similar feeling when they get the bill from his lawyers.

In August 1999 I visited with a very relaxed and cordial Anil Gandhy, who had been named Acting City Manager. He said The Bicycle Club had recently been sold and the contract of Chief Freeman had not been renewed.

Unfortunately, the city's problems are not over. In addition to the cost of the police department litigation, Bell Gardens will also have to deal with a claim for workers' compensation benefits filed by former Chief Freeman citing work related stress.

The City of Los Alamitos and Police Chief Michael Skogh have made an offered to settle the case against them. The case of Carter vs. Fred Freeman and the City of Bell Gardens is expected to go to trial in late 1999 or early 2000.

* * *

7

Operation Desert Snow

Beware travelers on Interstate 40. You are entering a war zone. If you look like the enemy, soldiers will find you, interrogate you, search your vehicle and if at all possible, arrest you and take your possessions.

The sleepy town of Needles, California, located 140 miles east of Barstow, got its name from jagged peaks which dot the surrounding Mojave desert. Often mentioned as the hottest city in the nation, Needles is also the birthplace of Operation Desert Snow. A distant outpost, it is a bunker in the war against drugs.

Like Gibraltar, Needles is strategically located. All motorists must pass to get themselves or their goods east or west. Travelers on Interstate 40, the successor to Route 66, must traverse the Mojave Desert before they see the fast food signs of Needles.

If you are a Caucasian with a few thousand dollars in your pocket on your way to Laughlin, Nevada, your luck will most likely be confined to the gaming tables. But, if you are a minority and fit the profile of the enemy, you may not get there. No signs warn that you are entering a place where the Fourth Amendment may not protect you.

In 1972, I was on my way to visit a customer in Virginia when I was pulled over by a young highway patrol officer. I had long hair, a beard and was wearing an African shirt. He must have thought I was the enemy. He was very up-tight and ordered me to follow him to the police station. I had never been targeted like this and I thought it was kind of interesting. I had nothing to hide, so I gladly showed my products to him. He searched my car and even called my bank to make sure I was legitimate. Maybe he thought I fit the profile of a money launderer too.

At the time, I just thought it was a new experience and I wasn't offended. I didn't use drugs and didn't have any, so it never dawned on me that drugs was what he was looking for. He didn't cite me and he finally did smile when I asked him how he liked my Moroccan leather products. I'm sure I'd feel differently if that happened all the time, but I guess I don't fit the profile anymore.

I am personally opposed to illegal drugs and as a matter of personal policy, I do not work on drug cases. My concern about what's happening in Needles is that the drug war is jeopardizing the freedom guaranteed by the Constitution. My specific concerns were addressed in an *LA Times* article published on February 11, 1996.

The article was written by Joseph D. McNamara, a 35 year police veteran and former Police Chief in Kansas City and San Jose. He is presently a research fellow at the Hoover Institution at Stanford University. His article, which is quoted verbatim, is excerpted for brevity:

Has The Drug War Created an Officer Liar's Club?
by Joseph D. McNamara

Are the nation's police officers a bunch of congenital liars?

Not many people took defense attorney Alan M. Dershowitz seriously when he charged that Los Angeles cops are taught to lie at the birth of their careers at the Police Academy. But as someone who spent 35 years wearing a police uniform, I've come to believe that hundreds of thousands of law enforcement officers commit felony perjury every year testifying about drug arrests.

These are not cops who take bribes or commit other crimes. Other than routinely lying, they are law abiding and dedicated. They don't feel lying under oath is wrong because politicians tell them they are engaged in a 'holy war' fighting evil. Then, too, the 'enemy' these mostly white cops are testifying against are poor Blacks and Latinos.

I became a New York City policeman five years before the Mapp Decision (1961). We were trained to search people who appeared suspicious. I questioned the apparent contradiction posed by the 4th Amendment, which guaranteed that people would be secure in their person and house from a search without a warrant. The instructor said not to worry. A suspect could sue in a civil action, but no jury would find against a cop trying to stop dope from being sold. He went on to say that if the courts really meant it, they wouldn't allow such evidence into a criminal trial. In its Mapp decision, the Supreme

Court cited this police attitude and the routine violations of the 4th Amendment as reasons enough to establish a national rule to exclude illegally obtained evidence.

Gradually, as police professionalization increased, police testimony became more honest. But the trend reversed in 1972 when President Richard M. Nixon declared a war against drugs and promised the nation that drug abuse would soon vanish. Succeeding presidents and Congresses repeated this false pledge despite evidence that drug use, drug profits and drug violence increased regardless of expanded enforcement and harsher penalties. Because the political rhetoric described a holy war in which evil has to be defeated, questioning police tactics was equivalent to supporting drug abuse.

Leaders of the drug war dehumanize their 'enemy,' not just foreign drug traffickers, but also American users. This mentality pushes the police into making ever more arrests... arrests that can only survive in court because of perjured police testimony. The fact that enforcement falls heavily on people of color also encourages illegal police tactics.

Non whites are arrested at four to five times the rates whites are arrested for drug crimes, regardless of the fact that 80% of drug crimes are committed by whites. The 'war' dehumanizes the cops as well as those they pursue.

The eroding integrity of law enforcement officers and the resulting decrease in public credibility are costs of the drug war yet to be acknowledged. Within the last few years, police departments in Los Angeles, Boston, New Orleans, San Francisco, Denver, New York and in other

large cities have suffered scandals involving police personnel lying under oath about drug evidence. Some officers in the New York City police and New York State police departments were convicted of falsifying drug evidence. Yet, President Bill Clinton appointed the heads of those agencies to be the drug czar and chief of the Drug Enforcement Agency, respectively, and they were confirmed in the Senate. The message that politicians seem to be sending to the nation's police chiefs is that we understand police perjury is a part of the drug war.

The vast majority of police forces are still being pushed into waging a war against drugs by politicians who ignore history and mislead the public into believing such a war can be won. Consequently, hundreds of thousands of illegal police searches take place and are lied about in court while drug war hawks pontificate about the immorality of people putting certain kinds of chemicals into their bloodstream.

END OF EXCERPT

CHP Officer Joe David developed a training program designed to conduct drug interdiction on Highway 40, which runs through Needles. He named this program "Operation Desert Snow" and he trains deputies on subjects ranging from who to search to how to find contraband. One of Joe David's students, Delbert Gray, graduated from the CHP Academy in 1986 and underwent additional training with the DEA and US Customs on how to spot a drug trafficker. One of the programs he trained with was Operation Pipeline. He now works as a patrol officer out of the Needles CHP substation.

Officer David, who patrolled with a canine and Officer Gray, who relies on his own devices, have an uncanny ability to locate illegal drugs. In 1997, Officer Delbert Gray testified that he had made over 400 narcotics arrests, seized over eight hundred pounds of cocaine, a thousand pounds of marijuana, fifty pounds of methamphetamine, assorted drugs and more than $1,000,000 in drug related cash.

Between them, Officers David and Gray keep the tiny Needles jail and Courthouse busy. A few years ago, the budget for this one courtroom facility was about $1.2 million for the year.

While the objective of these officers is laudable, someone needs to shed a bright light on their methods. In Needles, that someone is attorney J. Brian Campbell.

I first met Brian Campbell in 1992 when I handled a homicide case for an insurance company. A long haul trucker was facing charges in the death of a hitchhiker run over at one of the off ramps in Needles. Brian Campbell was appointed by the Court to defend him against vehicular manslaughter charges and, at the request of the insurance carrier, I became his investigator.

After numerous interviews and a reconstruction, we were able to show that the trucker, who was driving into Needles to eat, could not have seen the young male drifter. The hitchhiker was in the road and was caught by the rear wheels of the truck as it turned. We demonstrated that there wasn't anything the driver could do to prevent the tragic accident.

The homicide charge was ultimately dismissed, but while I was visiting Needles, Campbell told me about CHP Officers who appeared to be profiling minority drivers, then conducting pretext stops and criminal investigations. That was before the operation was known by name.

Brian Campbell gave up the rolling hills of upscale Palos Verdes Peninsula and opened a law practice in Needles in 1984. Nestled on the Colorado River near Arizona and Nevada, he's been one of only two attorneys in town. A devoted father of six, Campbell spends a lot of his personal time and resources trying to gather information regarding what he believes are unlawful practices by law enforcement.

The first generation son of Irish immigrants, Campbell credits his father with instilling in him a strong sense of equality under the law. Campbell told me that his father supported the family upon his arrival in the United States by selling Bibles door to door in the predominantly black neighborhoods of Los Angeles. His father described black families as warm, friendly and devoted and he taught his son that all men deserve equal treatment, the truth would always come out and a man should do what is right, regardless of the consequences.

Unfortunately, Campbell is greatly outmatched in this battle, but it doesn't look like he intends to give up. He continues to file motions whenever possible to make arresting officers answer to the court, and many continue to perjure themselves.

The California Highway Patrol claims that they do not keep track of the details and/or ethnicity of drivers who are stopped, so the only records available are those for the drivers arrested. On March 19, 1999, I called the supervisor of CHP Operations in Victorville, Sgt. Tom Carmichael, to request information regarding CHP policy and oversight guidelines. I left a message with a staff officer who said that Carmichael would be back in an hour. He returned my call five days later at 4:00 p.m. and I was not in. I returned his call the following morning, but he was not in. In a voice mail message I asked him to either page me or let me know when he would be in, but I've never heard from him.

With limited resources, Campbell has been able to learn a lot about the tactics used by Officers David and Gray. For instance, for each arrest they make, many innocent people are stopped, searched, then cited for a minor offense or simply released. These people most likely just want to get out of the area and never return, so we'll never know their stories.

Some documentation regarding drug interdiction efforts in the desert region has been obtained. These records indicate that each Operation Desert Snow officer should make 15 traffic stops per day. It is believed that two or three teams of five officers each work in the desert region on any given day. How can the command staff keep track of what their soldiers are doing if they are not required to record details on all of their stops?

Looking for Mr. Wrong

Officers David and Gray, leaders in the war against drugs, must be following orders. The problem is that in their treasure hunt for contraband, they seem to ignore the Constitution. They don't appear to look for Caucasians driving on Interstate 40. Officers David, Gray and others have testified that they have been trained in a program called "Operation Pipeline". They deny targeting minorities for traffic enforcement.

From the cases that he has handled, Campbell strongly believes that there are two different standards that apply to traffic stops by these officers and that the minority and out of state driver is subjected to a different speed limit, a different test for following too close and a different criteria for cracked windshields. In some cases, the officers fabricate the reason for a stop by indicating that they do not know the number of license plates required by different states.

These drug soldiers appear to be looking for "Mr. Wrong," who is described in the training textbook, "Tactics for Criminal Patrol" by Charles Remberg (Second printing -February 1996). This 509 page textbook and training manual describes the traditional profile taught to state traffic officers in "Operation Pipeline." On page 45, "Mr Wrong" is described as follows:

- "male Hispanics, blacks" or 'any swarthy, dark-haired outlander,' sometimes accompanied by a white female or a white male."

- "roughly twenty to forty-five years old."

- "possibly displaying an overindulgence in gold jewelry or other flamboyant style of dress."

- "often unshaven and unkempt in appearance."

- "traveling on an Interstate highway..."

- "driving a rental car with a Florida license plate, or a heavy, roomy 'road car,' often an older, two door General Motors model, possibly with heavily tinted windows but definitely with a commodious trunk, big natural 'dead space' cavities inside doors and quarter panels, powerful engine, and large capacity gas tank..."

- "hauling dope north or east and cash south or west..."

- "Frequently traveling at night, when cops are scarcer in many jurisdictions (virtually nonexistent in some), when darkness can camouflage personal features, and when vehicle searches are harder to conduct thoroughly and safely."

On page 47 of Tactics for Criminal Patrol, Remberg states (bold added):

"**But - the profile as a reliable absolute has been discredited. The full picture of who's out there with contraband today has grown much more complex than the profile suggests... if, indeed, it ever was quite that simple. 'It's a game.' explains one officer. The dopers have a strategy and we have a strategy. When ours gets better than theirs, they change.'**

Why is the Highway Patrol in Needles using and teaching

methods which are identified as having been discredited in the very book upon which they rely?

On page 50 of the same book, the author quotes "a how to book about being a successful smuggler offers pointers to couriers on avoiding the 'profile' look when traveling 'roads paved with bad intentions.' He quotes the following from this unidentified book (bold added):

- **"Learn the art of toning down (your) lifestyle. One problem the average smuggler has is that he lives his lifestyle: long hair, gold jewelry, fast cars, lots of girls. This creates problems..."**

- **"Dress is very important. Always wear good clothes, a dark suit or sport coat, and quality wingtip shoes. Buy a Rolex watch or a counterfeit Rolex watch. Be a business executive, not a devious planner. You are in the game for money, just like Exxon..."**

- **"Keep your hair short and your appearance neat and clean. One of the worst things you can do is look sloppy. Many smugglers are originally targeted by law officers because of appearance and flamboyant attire."**

END OF EXCERPT

Page 47 of Tactics for Criminal Patrol states:

"Profiling" Today

"To counter successful profiling, traffickers who hire mules have become shrewder and more eclectic. For "talent," they now recruit:

- *All* races, *All* ethnic groups, and *all* nationalities; the drug trade today offers equal opportunity employment. (One Midwestern Criminal Patrol team claims that about 80% of the drug couriers it finds now, including independent operators, are white;

- Clean-cut, all-American college students, attorneys, businessmen, even shady cops who "badge" their way out of any trouble;

- People who would never move a package normally but who've been laid off and need money;

- Grandma and grandpa who've been suckered into driving drug-loaded Winnebagos in "free trips" or hired outright as mules to supplement Social Security (the elderly, who tend to be virtually "invisible" to officers when they travel, are said to be the fastest-growing segments of transporters, the oldest on record believed to be an eighty-seven year old man caught with five kilos of coke);

- The disabled (including deaf people, who traffickers think will be treated leniently by police and whose difficulty in communicating is considered insurance against incriminating slips of the tongue);

- Juveniles ("When we had a lot of dope, the man gave us guns. I carried a .38," says a seventeen year old from Milwaukee who, along with others as young as thirteen, regularly delivered drugs in cars with hidden compartments);

- Women with children who rent themselves and their kids out to accompany men they don't know so a dope run will look like a "family outing" and be ignored by officers who are locked into traditional profiling. (Often there's a ten to fifteen year age difference between the male and the female, and the kids tend to be young, under six years. Women, in fact, have become like gold on contraband transports because many officers are inclined to be less suspicious of females..."

END OF EXCERPT

In a recent interview, attorney Campbell described the economic impact of repeated profile stops on minority drivers:

> "The average white person in society has a reasonable expectation that they won't be stopped without a valid reason. A traffic stop is often catastrophic for someone who is at a marginal economic level. Frequently, minorities have a suspended license because they were unable to pay a traffic citation. People often recover from these situations if they can stay employed and get the money together and not get stopped again."

Campbell described some of the troubling events which have happened in the Needles area:

- Albert Lewis, a black gentleman who drove a Cadillac with

Texas plates, was stopped two out of the three times he drove through Needles in a six month period. On both occasions he was driving the speed limit and he was stopped by the same officer, who had been traveling in the opposite direction. After the officer chased him down at a high rate of speed, he was questioned extensively and then released.

- A black family was detained on the road for an hour. They were in two separate cars and everybody in both cars was questioned. They were on their way to the southeast for the funeral of a grandparent.

- A farm worker was pulled over by a Needles police officer who had read Tactics of Criminal Patrol. The farm worker had some herbs in his glove compartment which the officer claimed was the drug, psilocybin. He also found a very small quantity of marijuana, reportedly "less than enough for one cigarette." The farm worker was arrested and when he was searched, his life savings of $8,212 in cash was found in his boots. When the lab report proved the herbs were not contraband, the charges were dropped, but the DA kept the $8,212 because the worker could not prove that the money was not proceeds from a drug transaction, even though this is not a requirement for amounts less than $25,000. After two years of needless litigation, he may soon get his money back, less legal fees. The cost of suing the DA for damages in a civil action would cost more than the amount in question. The DA's office uses this advantage to keep many assets to which they are otherwise not entitled.

- A black driver was pulled over after passing through the Agricultural Inspection Station on I-40 east of Needles. His car was searched and each Christmas present he had with him was unwrapped and inspected before he was released to try to have a merry Christmas.

- On March 4, 1997, Officer Gray pulled over two black females in a car from Michigan. The only reason Officer Gray gave for the stop was that he didn't observe a front license plate. Michigan is one of 21 states which issues only one plate. As an eleven year veteran of the highway patrol, Officer Gray should certainly know that many states issue only one plate.

At a hearing to suppress marijuana he seized as evidence, Officer Gray testified that he did not know Michigan issues only one plate and he did not check with dispatch to ask. The evidence was suppressed, but the DA re-filed the charges with a different judge.

During the above hearing, former San Bernardino County Deputy Public Defender Harry Hutchison asked Officer Gray if he knew whether Michigan requires one or two plates, to which Gray testified, "I don't know'. Hutchison then asked Officer Gray how California Vehicle Code Section 5200, which requires two plates, could relate to out of state plates. Officer Gray testified that he did not know whether or not the California Department of Motor Vehicles had ever issued a Michigan plate.

Under further questioning by Hutchison, Officer Gray testified that he is familiar with a book that contains every plate from every state on a one page 'cheat sheet,' but he did not have it with him when he made the stop. He also testified that he did not call dispatch to inquire how many plates Michigan requires.

Operation Desert Snow is offered as a training program to law enforcement organizations in other states. While I agree totally that we must do everything we can to identify and arrest drug traffickers, why stop only minorities? Could it be that they are the least likely to be heard in the event of a mistaken "hunch"? Why not stop and search every car, or at least every borders and it's quite possible more contraband would be found using this system.

Why violate the rights of minorities? Why not violate everyone's rights? The reason they can't is that the United States Supreme Court won't let them. In the case of State of Delaware v. Prouse (1979) 440 U.S. 648, 663, 59 L Ed 2nd 660, 673, 99 S. Ct. 1391, the Supreme Court held:

"... that except in those situations in which there is at least articulable and reasonable suspicion that a motorist is unlicenced or that an automobile is not registered, or that either the vehicle or an occupant is otherwise subject to seizure for violation of law, stopping an automobile and detaining the driver in order to check his driver's license and the registration of the automobile are unreasonable under the Fourth Amendment."

CHP claims that they do not keep track of the ethnicity of the drivers they stop, so Campbell decided to conduct his own study. On October 7th and 8th, 1996, surveillance expert Mike Wolivar and I monitored radio traffic and activity on highway 40 where it passes through Needles. Starting at dawn, we covertly videotaped as many CHP stops as we could. Using a rented car with an Arizona plate (Arizona is a one plate state), we started at 6:00 a.m. each day and recorded as much information as possible during the 8 hour shifts of the officers on duty.

On the first day, September 6, 1996, a video crew from the TV program "Real Stories of the Highway Patrol" was riding along, so we videotaped them videotaping the officers. The information obtained during our surveillance was used by a statistician to compile a report which determined that the number of Hispanics and blacks being stopped on those days was very disproportionate to the ethnic makeup of all drivers on Interstate 40.

I testified as part of a Motion to Suppress Evidence (PC

I testified as part of a Motion to Suppress Evidence (PC 1538.1) seized by Officer Gray. When Deputy District Attorney David Varman asked me how we conducted the surveillance, I explained that we monitored radio traffic, tape recorded all entries and videotaped all stops, some of them twice. DDA Varman was so surprised by my answer that he objected on the record to his own question. I had the video and audio tapes with me, but he didn't want to hear them. The motion was denied, but I think we got their attention.

In February of 1998, Judge Joseph Brisco presided over a similar hearing in Needles. In that case, Officer Gray was assisting Officer Blackwell with a felony arrest on Interstate 40 when a van with three black occupants passed his location. At the time he observed the van, he didn't notice any vehicle code violations. Nonetheless, he stopped what he was doing, rushed to his unit and pursued the van at about 100 miles per hour.

When he pulled the van over, Officer Gray claimed that they were following too close and they had a cracked windshield. In that case, contraband was found and all three occupants were arrested.

Deputy Public Defender Michael Kennedy filed a Motion to Suppress (PC 1538.1) the evidence seized by Officer Gray. At the hearing, the following exchanges occurred on the record:

THE COURT: Thank you, Mr. George. Well Mr. George, you are right, there is a considerable amount of contraband in this case. However, based on the evidence presented at this hearing, the Court is going to grant the Motion to Suppress as to Kenneth Harris and Charles Dorsey.

MR. CAMPBELL: Your honor, I'd ask to join at this time.

THE COURT: All right, Mr. Campbell has joined on behalf of Michael Harris. His motion is granted. All evidence in this case from the moment the vehicle was stopped, all defendants, all evidence seized will be suppressed.

MR. GEORGE: Motion to Dismiss; insufficient evidence.

THE COURT: Granted.

MR. KENNEDY: Thank you.

THE COURT: As to all defendants.

DDA VARMAN: Your honor, the People would inquire as to...

THE COURT: My reasons?

DDA VARMAN: Yes, please.

THE COURT: Be happy to tell you.

MR. KENNEDY: Well, I don't think it's appropriate to put expansive reasons on the record.

THE COURT: It's usually your side that wants to know.

MR. KENNEDY: Well, see, I'm looking at things two different ways depending on things. I think it's safer for everybody if reasons are not on the record--

THE COURT: I'd like to state them.

MR. KENNEDY: -- at this time.

THE COURT: I would like to state them.

(the defendants laughing)

MR. KENNEDY: None of that.

THE COURT: First of all--

MR. KENNEDY: No celebrating. No smiling.

THE COURT: Officer Gray testified that he was on a traffic stop on the eastbound lane of Interstate 40 somewhere around milepost 134 with Officer Blackwell. While at the side of the road, he noticed a mini van - I believe it was a green mini van - drove by at approximately 70 miles per hour. He looked up. He noticed that there were black or African American males in the vehicle. He did not testify that he noticed any vehicle code violations at that time. He did notice a crack in the window. He did not notice that the mini van--the green mini van, was traveling too closely behind a white van. He did not notice that there was a foot sticking up in the mini van. Nevertheless, he felt compelled to immediately leave the traffic stop that he was assisting Officer Blackwell on and get into his own vehicle to initiate a pursuit of the mini van. He didn't walk slowly to his car; neither did he run to his car. According to the testimony of two independent witnesses, Mr. Cox and Miss Sloma, he was somewhere between a walk and a run. But it appeared, in any event, it appeared to them that he was moving rapidly. He got into his patrol car and, by his own testimony, accelerated to somewhere in the neighborhood of a hundred miles an hour to overtake a car that had not violated any code vehicle code sections to his knowledge. And within a half mile pace, he decided he was going to pull that car over based upon a cracked windshield, which looking at Defendant's Exhibit A that's admitted, been admitted into evidence, clearly does not extend into the driver's side of the vehicle, so it couldn't have obscured the driver's vision. And he testified to the following too closely, as Mr. George pointed out, that's a very vague concept. What's too close?

The defendants, Mr. Harris and Mr. Dorsey, testified anywhere between eight to ten car lengths behind. If I recall Officer Gray's testimony from out first session, back on December 11th, he said something in the neighborhood of 40 feet. That's a wide discrepancy.

In any event, that was the basis for the stop, as much as I hate to say it, I think Mr. George's discussion of credibility has a lot of merit. I've listened to Officer Gray for three years now, and I've regularly noted, and in fact when I was reading this transcript to my wife last night, I made comments about the fact that he often answers:

"I could of, I may have. Maybe. Perhaps". He seems to have some aversion of giving a direct answer to a question. That troubles me a great deal, and it's gonna continue to trouble me every time he takes this witness stand.

And for these reasons, I do not believe that Officer Gray stopped this van because it had a cracked windshield, because it was following too closely, or because he saw a foot sticking out a window. I think his motivation was he saw a green van with three African American males in it and I think that's why he stopped it.

DDA VARMAN: Even though he stated otherwise?

THE COURT: That's right. I don't think Officer Gray was completely candid with this court, and that's the basis of my ruling."

END OF EXCERPT

After this ruling, the district attorney's office moved to disqualify Judge Brisco from hearing any cases in which Officer Gray is involved. They now allege that the judge is prejudiced against the People of the State of California.

In a recent interview, attorney Campbell provided some insight into the mind set of prosecutors in drug cases:

MADIGAN: The judge, by being courageous and finding in that one case that there was not sufficient cause to stop that car, now is being targeted by the DA's office?

CAMPBELL: The district attorney's office is saying he's prejudiced and basically they've put the rest of the judiciary in the county on notice that if they don't sit there and quietly acquiesce to the continuing pattern of perjury by this officer...

MADIGAN: They're asking them to participate in a conspiracy?

CAMPBELL: Essentially.

MADIGAN: The DA is saying, 'You go along and you get along,' otherwise we take away your livelihood?

CAMPBELL: They're saying 'We'll crucify you. We'll say that you're soft on crime."

MADIGAN: Are these judges elected?

CAMPBELL: Yes.

MADIGAN: Do you know of any particular things the DA does, in addition to papering the judge?

CAMPBELL: I believe there's a deputy district attorney, Gar

Jensen in Victorville, who has told me that he has attended almost every one of the Desert Snow courses offered by Joe David and he has audited that and he has provided training for those. That district attorney has told me that he does not believe it is unlawful for officers to stop minorities disproportionately, as long as they observe a vehicle code violation. I believe the district attorney's office has had some input into law enforcement that encouraged them to utilize this 'pretend' one license plate reason for stopping vehicles.

MADIGAN: Isn't this all patently dishonest?

CAMPBELL: Yes, it's dishonest to the core.

MADIGAN: And it's spreading to other areas?

CAMPBELL: Joe David testified over a year ago that he had taught in excess of fifteen thousand officers around the United States. The district attorney, Gar Jensen told me that he has put on programs all over the state of California, training officers for highway interdiction. He was originally funded from a grant. I don't know whether the grant was California or federal. These are things that need to be researched.

The book we have, <u>Tactics for Criminal Patrol</u>, which is a training manual, says that this training originally came from the federal government to tell state traffic officers that they should use the techniques that were effective at airport interdiction, basically stopping minorities.

At this point there's no way to tell fact from fiction in this "science" of drug interdiction. Because it's not a random sample. It's not a random polling. If we stop 80% minorities and then we find out that 80% of the drugs that we're aware of are being run by minorities, we don't know anything.

MADIGAN: But the number of trucks that go through, for example, each one of those trucks driven by a Caucasian, middle aged, heavy set driver could be carrying ten times the amount that someone would be able to carry in a false bottom in the trunk of a small vehicle driven by a minority.

CAMPBELL: I've heard of trucks being pulled over. They do pull over trucks.

MADIGAN: Are they pulling over minorities in the trucks?

CAMPBELL: Sometimes. I don't see enough truck cases to really form an opinion. But if you look at the number of people in this country, there's various studies published on what percentage of those people have used drugs. And what percentage have used them in the last month. Then you make some estimates based on that , in terms of quantity. There are huge quantities of drugs being transported all over this country, every day of the week. And into towns of every size, there's substantial quantities.

MADIGAN: But Joe David is a hero?

CAMPBELL: He's one of the heroes. Del Gray is a regular star on "Real Stories of the Highway Patrol." The head of the California Highway Patrol is the moderator of that show. Those film crews from Real Stories come out here and then they go other places. And if you watch that show and scrutinize it carefully, you'll see continuous violations of civil rights. When it comes to search and seizure, highway interdiction is primarily visited on minorities."

END OF EXCERPT

To The Victors Go The Spoils?

In San Bernardino County, the district attorney's office, whose expensively furnished offices are known as "mahogany row," shares in all assets seized in connection with drug cases.

The California Highway Patrol has reportedly authorized Joe David to market his training program. Law enforcement agencies across the United States are lining up to pay about $500 per officer to spend a few days at a hotel learning how to find drugs on the highways of America. Entrepreneur Joe David has testified that so far, he has trained more than 15,000 officers.

Documentation reviewed pertaining to the drug interdiction program in San Bernardino County indicated a target of 15 stops per day for each member of the interdiction team. If that happens, nearly a quarter million stops could be made each day. In a year as many as 56 million motorists could de subjected to the probing scrutiny of peace officers who are looking for an excuse to search their vehicles.

Minorities are all too familiar with the pretext stop while most Caucasians don't even know the problem exists. What's wrong with this picture?

The Message

If you are a minority and you want to go to the Colorado River, Lake Havasu or Laughlin, Nevada, fly to Bullhead City . . . and make sure the plane doesn't have a crack in the windshield!

***

Updates & Feedback

To find out what's happening in these cases or to let us know what you think, check our website:

www.twistedbadge.com